IT is about the Strategy

IT is about the Strategy

Strategy, Tactics and the Individual

Richard P. Skinner

Library of Congress Control Number: 2007903772

ISBN # 1-4196-6357-7

Publisher: BookSurge, LLC
             North Charleston, South Carolina

To order additional copies, please contact us.
BookSurge, LLC
www.booksurge.com
1-866-308-6235
orders@booksurge.com

What business and IT professionals are saying about
IT is about the Strategy

Richard Skinner's book <u>IT is about the Strategy</u> *puts into writing and action what many of us in the IT industry have thought and talked about for a long time. Richard's passion and guiding principles are a breath of fresh air. Making IT an "enabler" instead of a "barrier" is easier said than done, until you read the book!!*

Angelo Mazzocco
Chief Information Officer
Progressive Medical, Inc

<u>IT is about the Strategy</u> *is powerful. Richard Skinner's insights shift the conversation from technology problems to IT strategies for taking business to the next level. We give this book to our clients – they quickly see why their IT group is stuck and out of sync with their business goals. The leadership insight this book delivers is fundamental to a company's success.*

Robert Dorsey
President
R. DORSEY+COMPANY

<u>IT is about the Strategy</u> *is a very powerful book. Richard Skinner provides insight on how to take IT from a tactical function to the strategic aspect of organizations. I recommend this book to all professionals in leadership positions. It will change the way you think about IT.*

John Hrusovsky
Chief Executive Officer
GroundWork group

Amazing things happen when you have an IT strategy aligning business and IT objectives. Our business has grasped the concept that IT is not about the technology. IT is about the Strategy. With the aid of Richard Skinner's book, Dedicated Technologies has developed a strategic approach that enables us to eliminate the erroneous thinking. Richard has worked in Information Technology for 40 years. He knows his stuff! If you don't have an IT strategy then you need one now. Get the book and get started. This simple reading will bring lots of rewards to your organization.

> Patty Lickliter
> General Manager
> **Dedicated Technologies, Inc.**

Richard Skinner draws from his extensive practical experience to provide insight into the complex relationship between the business and Information Technology. IT is about the Strategy offers a unique perspective on the components of an effective IT strategy and why it must change as the organization grows and evolves. The emphasis on both business needs and the IT structure required to support them makes this a worthwhile read for anyone with leadership responsibilities in the organization.

> Blair Fujii
> Manager, Information Systems
> **Honda Trading America Corp.**

Richard effectively highlights how an enterprise can cope with its growing pains by identifying and focusing on strategy driven, value-add activities that maximize IT spend. We at TraverseIT use Richard's framework to help supplement our own strategy of Core IT vs. Chore IT, marrying such value-add activities with value-add products and services, in a way that always focuses on strategically maximizing client revenue, while reducing expenses. The book is a "must read!"

> Frank Guerino
> Chairman & CEO
> **TraverseIT**

Preface

This book is the first in a series regarding IT strategy and IT strategy execution (tactics).   The second book is titled simply *IT Tactics*.

Dedication

This book is dedicated to all of the IS employees and managers I have worked with throughout my career. Thank you for your understanding and patience while I talked incessantly about strategy.

A Word From The Author

This is the second release of this book. The primary difference between the first and second releases is the removal of the revenue guidelines and thresholds. The revenue thresholds proved to be less critical and relevant than other factors like business size measurements, the prior investment in technology, the size and maturity of the IS department and the business segment or industry. Based on feedback from IS and business leaders I was able to remove the revenue numbers thereby making the barriers and strategies more universally applicable. I also added the ten commandments chapter to summarize the important strategic principles.

Abbreviations

IT is simply Information Technology.

IS is simply Information Systems or Information Services.

SMB and SMBs are abbreviations for small- to medium-sized businesses and are the target audience for this book.

IT is about the Strategy
Table of Contents

Introduction

Objectives of the Book

The objective of this book is to provide strategic and tactical guidance and solutions for failing Information Services (IS) departments. Many IS departments in small- to medium-sized businesses (SMBs) are struggling to align themselves with the business and struggling to provide the proper level of technology service and support. These performance issues are not unique from business to business or from industry to industry. They follow a set repeatable pattern. Periodic failures on the part of the IS department are imminent and predictable. It is possible to understand how and when these failures will occur, to apply the proper remedies and to enable the business to deal effectively with these challenges.

The premise of this book is as follows: the decisions and expenditures that any business makes while growing their organization and the resulting ways that the business must construct and fund the IS department necessarily dooms IS to failure. These failure events are both identifiable and predictable. Each failure event is different depending on the size of the business at the time. Each needs to be dealt with strategically and tactically in different ways. Based on my industry experiences, I have identified three specific times when the IS organization begins to drastically fail the business. Using the proven remedies offered at each stage will enable the business to move forward and overcome the hurdles presented to the IS organization.

The content of this book consists of discussing these three failure events in detail and explaining how to deal with each effectively. The book will explain both the failures and the strategic and tactical approaches for dealing with them. The discussion will begin at small company start-up and continue with the company through several growth stages. Please reference appendix I.1 for a pictorial summary of these concepts and solutions. In the original version of this book I assigned revenue numbers to correspond to the barriers that will be reached. In retrospect I think that was counterproductive. Revenue numbers seem to vary widely and the barriers may just as well be a product of the age of the organization and the relative size of the IS department. My assertion is the same and I believe the three barriers described herein will be reached in succession no matter what the revenue base of the organization. This book will show how the things that make the business successful and enable it to grow are the very things that will force the IS department into failure.

The audience for this book is the SMB business leadership. This could be the CEO the CFO, the CTO, the CIO or another executive ultimately responsible for the IS department. The business and technology leadership will need to collaborate to make these exercises work.

Please note from the beginning that the premises and conclusions of this book have not been validated through scientific or organizational studies. To the best of my knowledge no such research has been conducted. The premises and conclusions are based solely on my experience and my personal anecdotal observations. I don't believe this invalidates my work in any way. I have been in the IS industry since its inception and have worked on every generation of computer hardware. This book reflects the knowledge and experience I have acquired during my forty years in IS.

The terminology I use may not be the terminology others are accustomed to using. Please allow me to define a few terms for the sake of this book.

Definition of Terms

Strategy

Strategy is defined as the vision and blueprint for the IS department. It is the critical and often-ignored segment of IS in many SMBs. Strategy provides the overriding direction and the governance for what gets done. Strategy encompasses taking a high-level view of the business and the IS department. It involves developing a framework from which to organize staff, build infrastructure, select appropriate technologies and engineer processes. It addresses overlying concerns about how to deliver IS services, how to organize the department, how to align with the business and how to define processes and procedures.

Strategy provides the basis for what gets done on a daily basis. It allows for technology selection and decision making. Using the often-quoted expression, if we don't know where we are going, any road will do. Thus, if we don't have a strategy, any approach and any technology can be used.

Tactics

Tactics are the resulting day-to-day execution of the strategy. These are the activities that support the vision and direction. Tactics are the way to realize the vision. The tactical segment brings the strategic planning and approach down to a specific set of activities and projects. It is the day-to-day application of tactical thinking that brings the strategy into focus. Tactics include personnel moves, project execution, system support activities and dealing with the business on a regular basis. Here we consider what needs to be done, how it is to be done, how to set expectations, how to standardize, how to measure and how to solidify the vision.

The Individual

The term "individual" refers to the way we manage and handle the human resources that are the key to supporting and executing the tactics. The individual segment brings the strategic and tactical work to the individual employee so they can reference it and be guided by it on a routine basis. The individual must do the work and so becomes the third major component in any IS department. It is critical to focus on recruiting and maintaining the proper staff while providing the proper direction and structure to them. Work here emphasizes team building and providing incentives to the staff to work toward a common goal and realize the vision. Each employee learns their role in the larger organization and how their contributions relate to it on a normal basis. It enables the associate and the manager to set expectations, define career goals, track progress and resolve issues.

Summary

A realistic and effective strategy will tie the three layers of strategy, tactics and the individual together so that the high-level vision affects the things that are done or not done on a daily basis. Only by tying together these three layers will the strategy have value.

The Business Layer Strategy   Chapter 1
Growth Level 1

1. *The way IS departments are funded and constructed in startup businesses assures IT failure.*

2. *Early on, the business must sacrifice structure and methodology for speed of delivery and immediate functionality.*

3. *Hackers make the business go.*

4. *Most early technology solutions are one-off or point solutions.*

5. *Few startups avoid the software development trap.*

6. *Sooner rather than later, the startup will be consumed by daily technology support.*

7. *Sooner rather than later, the startup will build an unsupportable technology mess.*

8. *Think strategy then tactics then the individual...not the reverse.*

I. INTRODUCTION

Our American business culture is famous for the small business startup. As a culture we revel in the entrepreneurial spirit and praise the entrepreneurs who start with a dream and a prayer, and build a thriving business. We stand in awe of their ability to invest little to nothing financially into the business; yet with blood, sweat and tears, they still construct a viable and profitable organization. It is a cornerstone of the United States economy and one of the reasons why the rest of the world admires and envies us.

This very phenomenon, however, dooms the IS departments in these SMBs to failure. There is simply no way over the course of the startup that the IS department can succeed. The way that small businesses are initiated, and the resulting way that the IS department is funded and constructed produces a failure. It is cause and effect. It automatically sets up a natural failure event at a specific point in time in the future of the IS department. We probably cannot find one SMB where this has not happened. The reason for this is as follows: the way that the business is built requires that the business sacrifice structure and methodology for speed of delivery and immediate functionality. It is not possible to invest in long-term, stable, lower total-cost-of-ownership solutions. The business must opt for short-term, unreliable and cheaper out-of-pocket ones. As the business grows these decisions will come back to haunt them. What small business out there today is not struggling with their IS department?

II. THE INDIVIDUAL

Let's look first at how the IS department is built. The first IS employee of any organization is always a hacker. He or she is a friend or a relative or the neighbor's kid, and always someone who has some PC experience and knows all of the buzzwords. He or she is always enamored with technology. This individual knows how to troubleshoot a PC and is known for helping friends and neighbors get connected and work with technology. This individual is usually looking for their start in the IS business, or already has their first job elsewhere and are frustrated by the bureaucracy and structure of a larger organization. This individual wants to tinker and experiment with technology. Quite simply, the first IS employee must always be a hacker. Let me state for the record that I use the term "hacker" not in a derogatory way but merely as a descriptor. Hackers are valuable and necessary people. Without them the average business could not get off the ground. While hackers do have an almost unnatural interest in technology, they can come up with some creative and impressive solutions by cobbling together technology components and delivering functionality that most businesses could not otherwise afford. Simply stated the business simply could not afford or succeed with anyone but a hacker. Anyone bringing more structure or less technology savvy to the business would simply not be useful.

III. TACTICS

A hacker is exactly what the business needs so that is where it starts. The first IS employee must be a dabbler in all things technological. The business will need phone systems, faxes, desktop computers, printing, basic networking, email, and accounting packages. The list seems endless. The business needs quick one-off solutions and there is no time for strategizing or worrying about tomorrow's connectivity requirements. The business will worry about those things if it gets to that point in the future. Survival is what it is all about. The business must have the bit of functionality today that enables it to get or keep a specific customer or a specific segment of business. The business can't worry about structure and methodology or selecting solutions that are scalable. The business can't spend for the future because the future is uncertain and the business doesn't have the money to buy the kind of technology that is really needed and that can be ultimately leveraged. The business has to land that next business opportunity and do whatever it takes from a technology support standpoint to make it work.

Let's start with a few real-life examples that I have experienced and that other SMBs will inevitably face.

- **Scenario 1 – A Print Job Opportunity**
  I worked for a startup organization that was nimble and responsive to their customers. One sales opportunity was a custom print job that was required annually and could bring three million dollars of revenue into the company. The business was not currently providing any other related print solutions. The decision was made to go forward with the sale. Then the business had to

figure out how to deliver. There were basically two options. Option one was to buy a printing software package with all the functions and features. It would simply require some initial setup and configuration. Option two was to develop the print capability from scratch using disparate but free or cheap components. The printing software package, option one, was flexible and would handle this job and many others like it. The problem was that it was a major investment of thousands of dollars and would cut deeply into the profit margin. Also, there was no guarantee that the printing job would be an ongoing product or ever sold again. The second option was to use freeware and shareware to cobble together the print solution from scratch. The second solution would also be brittle and would require numerous manual interventions to run and constant repairs and maintenance to support. It would require hours and hours of running each of many steps by hand and conducting manual quality assurance activities against the output of each step. Which solution do you think the SMB chose? Which would a normal business choose? If the business chooses the second option and printing becomes a major part of the business, does this not set the IS department up for failure?

- **Scenario 2 – Email Solution Required**

    The startup company I worked for needed email to communicate internally and with clients. The business could not do business without it. The permanent and robust choice would be to use industry standard Microsoft and install an Exchange server with Outlook and other out-of-the-box capabilities. The cost of an Exchange server is a substantial investment (thousands of dollars), and will wreak havoc with both the financial picture and the cash flow. The IS resource is a creative and resourceful hacker. He feels he can develop the email capability using freeware and shareware for several hundred dollars in just a few days. The solution, however, will be somewhat primitive and will have little to no security or virus protection. It will require daily management and maintenance and will have some relatively minor reliability issues. Which direction do you think the business took? Which way would your business go? If the business does continue to thrive and grow has this set the IS department up to fail?

- **Scenario 3 – A Telephone System Solution**

    The startup can't live without basic telephone service. The business can't even pretend to do business without this critical connection to the outside world. A small, new or reconditioned, state-of-the-art key system from an industry leader will cost tens of thousands of dollars. The only alternative is to shop elsewhere and buy an off-brand on the used market for thousands of dollars. The industry leader offers 100 percent availability and uptime with user training and support. There will be numerous internal features like conferencing, call forwarding, and programmed hunt groups. The used and nonstandard solution will require that one of the IS team read the manuals and self-teach to do the installation, configuration, and support. The used solution can also be supported on a time-and-materials basis by a third party but you are on the bottom of the priority list with no response time guarantees. It will also provide only basic dial tone with no additional available features. The choice is between basic cheap functionality with heavy ongoing maintenance and support costs and costly full-featured functionality with little to no ongoing support costs. It is the classic case of pay me now or pay me later. What choice did they make? Which choice would your business make? If the business grows have we set the IS department up for another failure?

Slowly but relentlessly, as our examples indicate, the business spends more money on technology and more on one-off and point solutions. One-off and point solutions solve a specific but narrow technology or business problem but provide nothing to build on or leverage. The business is cobbling together a technology solution set only in the strictest sense of the word.

The business exhausts the time of the single individual in IS. The business goes to the sole IS resource, the existing hacker, and asks them what kind of help is needed. Naturally the response will be that the business needs another one of them. So the business hires a second hacker, and a third, and so on. Eventually the business has six to ten hackers all with the same background and skill sets. All are able to slam in quick technology solutions and all are able to code and configure and tinker. Something else happens naturally as well. The business starts to spend more and more time and more and more money on day-to-day support. With every piece of technology that gets installed the business must dedicate more manpower to support it. This is a truly hidden cost to the business and one that is not often understood. Technology does not just run itself. It requires constant care and feeding. The IS department must apply upgrades and patches. They are constantly making changes and with changes come instability and outages. The IS department has no time to spend on cleaning up the interfaces between technologies so the interfaces are problematic and, therefore, will break. The IS department has no time to set up batch scheduling or automatic processing. Everything, including production and services to key clients, is run by hand and must be continuously monitored, tweaked and nudged. Everything is person-dependent and not process-dependent. The business does not even recognize that they have processes yet. The IS department has people scrambling around trying to keep the technology up and working while responding to the customer crisis of the day. They have written nothing down so there is no documentation, procedures, or instructions. Everything is in somebody's head.

By this time the business will also get into some software development. This is a key moment in the evolution of the business that will, in all likelihood, go unnoticed. All small businesses could avoid this costly mistake but few seldom do. This is the software development blunder. Let's use the accounting software as an example but the same mistakes will most likely be made for every other software area that gets addressed. The business has now outgrown Quicken or some other smaller software package and must consider an upgrade. Maybe the business has added too many clerks or accounting assistants. In any case, the business is now having trouble knowing their financial state, closing at month end, and getting the information that allows leadership to be proactive instead of reactive. The business has to do something.

The accounting group will claim that there is no accounting package out there that does everything the business needs. This may not be accurate. Alternately, they will tell you that a specific package they have used elsewhere will work but the IS department will have to modify it somewhat. This will not be accurate. So the business takes the plunge and decides to build from scratch or, worse yet, buy a package and make wholesale modifications to it. The secret here is that the business has chosen to modify software to meet existing business processes instead of modifying existing business processes to conform to the software. In most cases the software will not be flawed—the processes will.

The IS department staff should also be counted on to keep the business from making this mistake but they will not. IS employees live to build things. Coding a new application is fun and challenging… at least until documentation and implementation time. So the IS department will start coding and begin a cycle of delays and disappointments. Eighty percent of all software development projects fail, even in larger organizations. The application may never be fully functional and, if delivered at all, will start a cycle of maintenance and enhancement that will drain IS and company resources, time, and money. As I will explain later in this book, software development should be avoided at all costs unless it gives the business a distinct competitive advantage.

By now the IS department will resemble the plate-spinning comedian on the old Ed Sullivan show. It will be a constant game of trying to keep the numerous plates spinning (read technology up and available) and not falling in succession to the floor (read technology crashing). Most of the daily activities for members of the IS team will be trying to keep the infrastructure up and functioning, the phones working, the email flowing, the accounting reports generated, and the desktops free of failures and viruses. All forward progress will grind to a halt and customers will naturally begin to suffer.

IV. STRATEGY

Strategically, where are we now? The business has started to grow and revenues are up but all is not well within the technology arena. The IS department is no longer an asset but an impediment to the organization. This is inevitable. For the most part technology will be unstable. The IS department has slammed in solution after solution with no thought to scaling or integration. The solutions solved a specific business problem or two, but in the larger scheme of things they were not building blocks or part of a strategic solution set. The business will have the IS employees running around trying to keep technology up and available. IS support costs have grown geometrically with the number of solutions IS has slammed in place. There are no economies of scale. The business went for low-cost or no-cost solutions and these require daily care and feeding. Nothing seems to run unattended. There are no schedules for anything, and maintenance and support has become difficult. Each day is an adventure and a series of outages and breakdowns. There is no documentation and everything exists only in the IS people's heads. No interfaces exist. Nothing talks to anything else. Most of the technology decisions that were made were right at the time but are wrong for now. The business will feel blocked and stymied.

At this point in time, the business will recognize that the IS department doesn't have a strategy and that they don't know how to define one. IS is stuck in a spending and patching cycle that has the business questioning all aspects of the technology. The business relationship with the IS team has gone sour. They are working hard but getting few results. They are a hindrance to the business and not an asset. The business has officially reached growth barrier 1.

V. SUMMARY

In summary, business leadership recognizes that they now have the wrong approach, the wrong staffing, and the wrong skill sets to break through the barrier ahead. The business leadership is questioning how this could have happened since this is the team and approach that got the business here. This team and this approach were terrific. Through their efforts the business has gotten to this growth level. And that is the specific point of this book. The business and IS has reached the point where what it did to get here has set it up for failure. What worked before and made the business successful no longer works. It is time to regroup, step back, and take a fresh look at the challenge.
It is worth noting that I structured this section to follow the sequence:

- Individual
- Tactics
- Strategy

This is the reverse order in which it should have flowed. The order is reversed because this is the sequence in which the business must approach technology to get the business off the ground. It is a natural and normal approach. There will seldom be variance. I feel this first barrier may be encountered by the business when revenues are as low as twenty-five million or as high as several hundred million. It will vary by industry and by the dependence on technology within the business. It will also vary based on the number of IS employees, the amount of investment by the business in IT, and the size of the company. Whatever the situation, the business has now hit this critical first barrier and the question becomes how the business is going to deal with it.

Overcoming Growth Barrier 1
Business Layer Strategy

Chapter 2

1. *The business layer strategy overcomes growth barrier 1.*

2. *Divide and conquer. Separate all technology into three layers.*

3. *The layers are infrastructure, back office applications, and customer facing applications.*

4. *The business strategy drives the IT strategy.*

5. *First identify the layers and the technologies within.*

6. *Next assess strengths and weaknesses by layer.*

7. *Then write strategic statements by layer.*

I. INTRODUCTION

This approach, executed properly, is guaranteed to get the business past the IS challenges encountered at the first barrier. Please reference appendix 2.1 for an overview of the strategy and tactics required for this approach. The business should use the strategy and tactics appropriate for the size of the business at this point in time. The strategy and tactics will serve the business well until it reaches the next barrier. By the way, if there was a way to avoid the next barrier, I would prescribe it as well. I do not feel that a way exists. The resources and funding that are available for supporting technology in most SMBs will not allow the business to totally avoid the next barrier. However, using this approach, the business may minimize the negative impact.

The work to be done by the business at this stage is to develop the strategic IS direction using the business layer approach. The business layer approach entails categorizing the technology solutions into one of three layers and addressing each of these layers in a different strategic way. Once the layers are defined and the strategy is set the business will develop a series of projects to align the technologies within the layers…thereby executing the tactics. All of this will be described in a narrative form below with very little need for charts and graphs. The IS department must also realign the IS manpower resources in order to be successful. The prescribed model will enable the business to move the IS resource from a reactive technology-centric group to a proactive business-centric team focused on customers. Here are the steps in the business layer approach.

II. STRATEGY

A. Assessment

It is a natural beginning to first formally document where both the business and the IS department reside today. The IS department needs to have a baseline from which to execute and measure their progress. These exercises need to be formal and structured but not exhaustive or comprehensive. Speed of delivery is critical.

B. Business Assessment

Before the business can define where the IS resource must go, the IS department must know where the business is going. Before the business can define where the business is going, we must know where the business resides today. Usually the business leadership and most of the business employees can supply a coherent view of where the business resides today. The critical exercise is to look at the state of the business today in terms of problems, limitations, and inhibitors brought on by IS. While most but not all of these will be technology related, the ones that are can be addressed by this exercise.

1. Technology Challenges

This exercise is the simple step of defining the problems and issues surrounding technology and the business. This can be as formal as a narrative in a published report or as informal as a series of bullet points in an email. What is critical is to document the problems all in one location so that business leadership can assure that they are addressed and resolved by the resulting strategy. The identified issues will need discussion, refinement, and publication for all to see. Remember the business is not finding fault with the IS team. These breakdowns are normal, natural, and unavoidable. The IS department, when engaged, must put egos aside and clearly assist in defining the problems so they can be addressed. These definitions should be stated in the context of what business functions are impacted. Here are a couple of sample problem statements that can be used to define the technology challenges:

- External email stops functioning at least once a week. We have no idea that it is broken because we cannot detect the absence of getting external email. We depend upon email for customer orders and the exchange of photographic proofs. If we mishandle or ignore orders, we not only jeopardize that specific order but the ongoing client relationship.
- The interface between our web orders and our web fulfillment is manual. There are numerous manual steps that must be executed to fill an order and these steps are subject to human intervention and failure. Also, since all of the tracking is manual, we are constantly losing track of inventory and must do weekly physical inventory counts to keep inventory in stock.

- The accounting server reboots itself at least once a day. This has been going on for several weeks. When it reboots we lose whatever transactions we were working on and sometimes previous transactions. It takes up to an hour to reconfirm what we did and whether the transactions were processed. The IS group can only tell us it is a hardware glitch; they can't seem to fix it.

2. Business Direction

Next the IS department must know the business plans. This is the step that reinforces the critical need to resolve the technology problems. It will also provide the IS leadership with the business vision. The business leadership and the IS leadership need to conduct a reasonable—and likely prolonged—dialogue to communicate where the company is headed. The questions below should foster some initial discussion. An SMB that has done some formal planning should be able to readily provide this information.

- What businesses are we going to continue to be in? What are the identified lines of business? Should we expect changes in our current direction?
- What is the market like? What is the revenue potential in the marketplace? What is our market share and how are we perceived in the marketplace?
- What are the company goals as far as revenues (dollars), profitability (margins, profits, EBITA in dollars) and resulting number of employees (size)?
- How are we going to grow (approach)? Are we going to grow through acquisitions, franchising, geographic expansion, or centralized growth?
- What locations are we planning to be in and where might these locations be or how might they be chosen? Geographically, where are we going to do business?
- Do we have goals of sales or production facilities in other locations or states? Where are specific facilities anticipated to be located?

C. Technology Assessment

Now that the business has documented the company status and business direction in relationship to the IS department, the next challenge is to align IS with the business and, using the guiding principles and tactics given below, chart the course for IS.

1. Identifying the Layers

The strategy requires that the business takes a different view—a fresh look, if you will—at the business and the associated technologies used to support the business. First classify each of the existing technologies into one of the categories below. There are several ways to get started with this exercise. The business could start with a broad list of all technologies. They could take a department by department view and list the technologies used by each department. (This may provide additional value later as well.) Last, the business could also use some of the samples I give below and expound on them. Please reference appendix 2.2 for a pictorial representation of this exercise.

a. Base Layer – Infrastructure

This is the base layer of technology that consists of the underlying infrastructure on which all other functionality is built. It is the foundation. It includes things like local and wide area networks, telephone systems, work stations or PC desktops, processors and servers, printers, and other miscellaneous hardware. This layer is a surprisingly common layer that will not differ much from SMB to SMB.

b. Middle Layer – Back Office

This is the middle layer of technology that is critical to the day-to-day running of the company and provides the applications and functionality that nearly all SMBs cannot live without. It resides and functions on top of the infrastructure layer. It consists of applications that provide managerial support, administrative support, and office systems. It includes accounting packages, financial packages, human resource systems, email capabilities, voice mail functionality, document faxing and handling, and most other internal software and application systems. This layer is also a surprisingly common layer that will not differ much from SMB to SMB.

c. Top Layer – Products and Services

This is the top layer of technology. It is what makes each business unique. It is specific to the business and enables the business to do what it does to make money. It is the customer facing and customer servicing systems and solutions that support existing clients or enable the business to secure new clients.

d. Summary

Using this approach the business will now have an exhaustive list of all technology solutions. It is important not to get hung up on technologies or systems that may seem to fall into one layer or another. The business should slot the system based on best guesses and move on. What might be a back office technology for one business could very well be a customer facing technology for another. By definition, if it touches the customer in a meaningful way then you can classify it as a customer facing technology. Remember that these layers build from the bottom to the top as in any form of construction. As a general rule the business can classify the layers in terms of whether they provide core functionality or a competitive edge to the business. The guideline to use is to buy or outsource for core functionality and build or in source for a competitive edge. In most cases the business should clearly outsource (as much as possible) the technology infrastructure and back office systems and in source customer facing products and services. It is critical that the business cultivate the internal IS staff to focus on customers.

2. Assessment by Layer

Now the business must match the technology problems or issues identified in the business assessment to the technology layers. Some problems will fit into multiple layers and should be duplicated in each location so as not to be missed. Flag these with an indicator showing the entire problem is not in a single layer. Matching up the identified problems with the individual layers will enable the business to see where the problems should be addressed and what strategy should be used to address them. Each layer will have a different strategy.

a. Base Layer

In the infrastructure layer, the business leadership needs to task the IS leadership with providing a narrative describing what the technology does for the business. This can be very basic but should be couched in business terms. Use the identified technology problems and issues to expand on the documentation for the identified technologies. In order to address issues the IS department and the business must have the technologies clearly defined and charted. Expand the layer chart to include these problems and issues.

b. Middle Layer

In the second, or back office layer, the business and IS leadership should perform the same descriptive and slotting exercises. Here the business leadership needs to use the IS leadership to document whether it has been buying or building solutions. IS leadership should also document as much information as possible about each component including, but not limited to, the following:
- the date the application was implemented
- the amount of maintenance and support required
- vendor relationships and support provided
- versions available versus version installed
- interfaces and interactions with other applications
- how committed or dedicated the business is to these legacy applications

c. Top Layer

In the third, or customer facing layer, the business needs to use the IS leadership to perform the same descriptive and slotting exercises. In addition to the issues, document the following for all customer facing applications:
- status regarding purchased or home-grown
- stability of the application
- functionality, including weaknesses of the application
- maintenance and support issues
- competitive issues with the application within the marketplace
- general feeling about the application by the business

These are the systems and applications the business should be focusing on and they should be stable, scalable, and robust. Most likely these systems are in the same troublesome state as the previous two layers.

d. Summary

The business now has a "state of the business" report and a "state of the IS department" report that will be used to define a strategy and map a direction.

D. Strategic Statements

Using the reports from the three layers above, the business (with the assistance of IS) can now generate a basic strategy for each layer that will allow it to fast-track progress. The business and IS leadership can jointly translate the strategy into tactics by identifying the projects that will be executed to remedy the existing problems and propel the business in the required direction. The business leadership will now be able to address some problems in each area immediately by running some concurrent projects. However, it will ultimately require that the business and IS leadership implement and solve in the infrastructure layer first, followed by the administrative layer, then the customer facing layer. Remember, this is about construction and the business must build from the bottom to the top.

Let's review a few sample strategic statements.

1. **Base Layer**

    -   **Local Area Network** - Our local area network will connect all internal users to all existing and future technologies based on need. The network will approach five nines (.99999) in availability and will be robust enough to handle any internal data traffic or file transfers. The network will be secure and hardened.
    -   **Desktops** - Our desktops will have a minimum configuration based on user needs that will be defined during subsequent meetings. We will replace desktops every three years and laptops every two years. We will have a standard desktop configuration which will not be modified without the consent of the head of IS. No external software will be loaded without written permission and documented business need. Every desktop will have the standard Microsoft operating system and office suite, and will be fully licensed.

2. **Middle Layer**

    -   **Accounting System** - Our accounting system will be a purchased package that will not be modified. It will be configured and enhanced only by the vendor. It will meet all of our published requirements. It will interface seamlessly with our commission system and our warehouse management system. It will allow us to proactively manage the business and provide extensive ad hoc reporting capability.

- **Commission System** - Our commission system will be a purchased package that will not be modified. It will be configured and enhanced only by the vendor. It will handle our unique commission split structure and allow for four levels of hierarchy within the sales force. It will provide for interfaces to the sales and lead tracking systems as well as the payroll component of our benefits package system. If the package will not support a specific commission structure, we will not pay in that manner. We will find other ways to accomplish the same compensation.

3. **Top Layer**

- **Call Center and Agent Call Handling** - Our call center will be constructed using only state-of-the-art components and industry leading vendors. Our call center will allow for voice conversations and web chats. It will offer skills-based routing and the ability to record and capture every call including the system data component. It will provide standard daily reporting which will be defined in subsequent meetings.
- **Customer Printing** - We will print any document for any customer at any time. We will print color as well as black. We will print on any size paper. We will attempt to provide twenty-four-hour turnaround on reasonable volumes. We will allow our customers to submit print data in any form and will convert it to our standard print format. We will make it easy for our customers to engage us.

III. Summary

This approach offers a truly unique view of the business and allows the business to begin construction of IS infrastructure and solutions from the ground up. This is powerful stuff!

Business Layer Tactics

WISDOM to work by:

1. *Tactics bring the business layer strategy to fruition.*

2. *Follow the recommended tactics by layer.*

3. *Remember, there is no competitive advantage in the infrastructure or back office layers.*

4. *Problems in the infrastructure or back office layers can keep you from competing and from staying in business but cannot differentiate you in the marketplace.*

5. *Strategically define where the business needs to go (by layer).*

6. *Tactically define how the business is going to get there (guidelines and guiding principles).*

7. *Identify and execute the resulting projects.*

I. INTRODUCTION

This is the second component of the business layer approach and consists of strategy execution—what I would define as tactics—and states exactly what the business is going to do.

II. TACTICS

A. Base Layer – Infrastructure

Here are the tactics I recommend. First and foremost, please keep the following principles in mind and do not deviate from them:

- **Buy instead of building**
  The business should outsource the work to independent external integrators and not hardware vendors. Hardware vendors are in the market to sell products while external integrators are paid to integrate products from multiple vendors. External integrators can choose products from the hardware vendors most suitable to the challenge at hand. The business should not ask or allow the IS

department to build infrastructure. For example, the IS department should not build the local area network using internal staff. Instead hire an independent integrator and use internal staff for vendor relationship management and executing the vision. There is no value and no competitive advantage in this layer. The IS department should not need or want to become proficient at building infrastructure. Nothing the business can do here will provide it with a competitive edge.

- **Adopt industry standards**

    This is very important! Nothing is more expensive than fork-lifting out old solutions. This happens when the technology vendor goes out of business, or when the business cannot get support, or when support is so expensive it is cheaper to replace the technology. The ultimate solution is to do solid market research, identify the industry leaders, and make safe choices. I would recommend the business stay the middle ground. It is dangerous to get ahead of the technology curve and buy "bleeding edge" technology. Make every effort to select a vendor who will be in the market for the long term.

- **Think connectivity and interfaces**

    It is important that each business or technology system connect seamlessly and "talk" or communicate with every other one. The IS department can spend a substantial amount of time trying to build these interfaces after purchase or they can be accommodated during the planning phase. It is important to define connectivity as an up-front requirement in dealing with integrators. The integrators can meet this need if the business can adequately define it. Outsourcing does not absolve the business of making choices. If anything it requires that the business define the requirements more closely and have a clearer picture when it starts.

    Feel free to use this checklist to develop a project list:
    - Work stations, PCs, Desktops
    - Printers
    - Internet and Intranet
    - Local Area Network
    - Wide Area Network
    - Fax
    - Processors and Servers
    - Telephone System

Using the layer diagram, the technology descriptions, the slotted problems and issues lists, and these principles, business leadership can develop the infrastructure vision. The projects will naturally fall out from the vision. Prioritize these projects based on factors including the strongest positive business impact, the cost to the business, and the available manpower. Please remember that these are business projects and not technology projects. The business and the IS department should seek only to manage this vision and not specialize or become experts in any area of infrastructure unless it is ultimately a component of the customer facing suite.

B. Middle Layer – Back Office

To begin almost everything discussed in addressing the base layer holds true for the middle or back office layer. Instead of hardware infrastructure, the business is dealing with primarily software and application systems with a smattering of hardware components as well.

Surprisingly the middle layer or back office strategy in one SMB will also not differ substantially from most other SMBs. The same components are required for all businesses since all businesses have the same accounting, payroll, human resource, and communication requirements. As with the base layer there are three simple principles which are nearly the same:

- **Buy instead of building**

  The business should outsource the work to independent external application or software integrators and not specific software vendors. Software vendors are in the business to sell software. Software integrators can be vendor independent and choose from the many available solutions. More importantly, the IS department should not be allowed to build it themselves. For example, the business should never buy a software package and internally make modifications. The business should buy and use the functionality provided. I recommend changing the business processes to meet the demands of the software, not the reverse. If the business collected the requirements properly, the package should suffice. If not, consider starting over and redoing the requirements. Reinstallation is preferable to continual unbridled modification. It is also preferable to hire an independent integrator who markets numerous products and use internal staff for vendor relationship management and executing the vision. Again there is no value and no competitive advantage in this layer. The business and the IS department do not need or want to become adept at building this layer. Nothing the business can do here will provide a competitive edge.

- **Adopt industry standards**

  As in infrastructure this principle is extremely important. The only thing more expensive than reinstallation of back office solutions is making modifications to them. It is preferable to do market research and identify the industry leaders. Make safe choices. It is important to define the business requirements and use a structured selection process. The business should not allow any one person to drive any one selection process. Please try to avoid buying based on salespeople or sales relationships. Visits to existing clients using the back office solution being investigated are recommended. Use a scoring system and try to be fair and impartial. Try to select a vendor who will be in the market for the long term and who can support and enhance their products.

- **Think connectivity and interfaces**

  It is critical that the back office systems connect seamlessly and "talk" or communicate with each other. The IS department can spend a substantial amount of time trying to construct these interfaces after purchase or these can be accommodated in the planning phase. It is important to define connectivity as an up-front requirement in dealing with integrators. The integrators can meet the need if the business can adequately define it. Outsourcing does not absolve the business of making choices. If anything it requires that the business define the requirments more closely and have a clearer picture when it starts. Keying data from system to system is a very bad practice. There is usually an inverse relationship between the number of databases or spreadsheets and the up-front work done on connectivity and interfaces. Every manual interface is an opportunity for a mistake. Buying a suite of products that do not integrate can ultimately be as expensive as building solutions internally.

Feel free to use this checklist to develop a project list:
- Accounting
- General Ledger
- Accounts Payable
- Accounts Receivable
- Fixed Assets
- Financial Statements
- Payroll
- Benefits
- Human Resources
- Sales and Lead Tracking
- Commissions
- Advertising
- Document Management (imaging, repositories)
- Customer Relationship Management

Using the layer diagram, the descriptions, the slotted problems and issues lists, and these principles, the business can develop a back office vision. The projects will naturally fall out from this vision. Prioritize these projects based on the strongest positive business impact, the cost to the business, and the available manpower. Remember, these are business projects and not technology projects. Seek only to manage this vision. Do not specialize or become experts in any area of the back office unless it is ultimately a component of the customer facing suite.

The IS department may find that they have nothing to start with in the back office suite that can be reused. The choices that were made to meet the daily challenges were not well thought out and, unless the IS department got lucky, are not meeting the needs of the business. Resist the impulse to build anything. The business leadership must buy into the mantra that it will modify the business processes to meet the software and not modify the software to meet the business processes. These processes change with personnel changes anyway.

Select industry leaders and stick with them. Industry leaders do not necessarily have the best solutions; they just have the best marketing and sales departments. Their products do work. There are no guarantees but industry leaders usually put more capital into product development, provide better support, and are more likely to stay in business. Niche players usually fit the opposite profile.

Consider these "black boxes" and keep them away from the IS department as much as possible. Use the independent integrators to the fullest extent. Cultivate vendors. Look for products that are multifaceted, have extensive capabilities, and interface with their own vendor's packages and other packages. Buy a lesser-featured but integrated product as opposed to a better-featured stand-alone one. Integration is rife with frustrations and disappointments. The fewer the solutions and the fewer the interfaces that are built between systems, the fewer problems will be experienced. The business should not be too afraid to tie itself tightly to one vendor offering a wide suite of products. The business is looking for business functionality and not a competitive edge.

Look for solutions that save steps. Buy electronic faxing and fax servers instead of paper fax machines. Buy the best you can afford. The business doesn't need problems with communications so invest wisely. Keep the accounting and finance simple. Stay with the package. If the business has to enhance reporting, strive to use industry standard tools so that experts are always available.

Acquiring and using reliable and scalable back office systems takes knowledgeable industry partners, careful planning, adequate time, and serious investments in industry standard solutions. There is no competitive advantage in the back office solution suite. It is best to think of it as the cost of doing business. The business needs to do it right the first time and put it behind them.

C. Top Layer – Customer Facing Products and Services

This layer is where the business can differentiate itself. While outsourcing, standardizing, and basically homogenizing the first two layers, the solutions here need to be unique and creative. These are the systems that are customer facing and support the delivery of products or services, whichever is the core reason for being in business. Here is where the business needs to be creative and differentiate itself. These are the systems that support the existing client base or enable the business to secure new markets or new clients. This is where the business can consider custom development and creative solutions. The IS department does not have to build systems here. In many cases there are packages that do what needs to be done. If the business is looking for competitive advantages in the marketplace it may be found in new development. If at all possible avoid having the IS team sit down and start coding. Coding systems from scratch should almost never be done anymore. The IS department needs to be systems facilitators who select existing components or existing tool sets and make them work together in new and unusual ways. Most likely the business cannot afford the time frames required for simple custom software development.

- **Consider building**

  The IS department may well be able to find products and services in the marketplace to do basic functionality but here they may consider building before buying. Still try to avoid total custom development. Custom development is very expensive and historically 80 percent of all software development projects fail. Try constructing systems with components or building blocks instead of coding. Try developing custom applications with tool sets such as work flow, document management, messaging tools, and other engines or components. The business can still find a competitive edge in the creative use and application of some of these products.

- **Remember the interfaces to the back office applications but emphasize customer facing functionality**
  Consider the flow of data out of customer facing systems into billing, receivables, and other accounting and financial systems. These interfaces could become customer issues if the interfaces fail or otherwise become inaccurate or unreliable. Do not let these become overriding concerns but document them as requirements and try to address them.

- **In source by developing internal support capabilities**
  Here is where the IS department can turn the hackers loose again. This is where their creativity and technology savvy will pay dividends. Since the business has avoided committing the internal IS department's time, energy, and effort to the first two layers, the business can commit to differentiating the business from the competition. The competition is having the same challenges and problems. They got here the same way. There is no escaping this trap. How the business deals with this challenge, at this point in time, will determine whether the business stays in the pack, falls along the wayside, or forges ahead and leaves the competition behind.

Using the layer diagram, the descriptions, the slotted problems and issues lists, and these principles, the business can develop a customer facing vision. The projects will naturally fall out from the vision. Prioritize these projects based on the largest positive business impact, the return on investment to the business, and the available manpower. Remember that these are business projects not technology projects. Seek only to manage this vision. This is the layer to become experts in the technologies and find ways to develop or integrate solution sets to develop that competitive edge.

III. SUMMARY

What we have learned to do is:
- Strategically define where the business wants to go (by layer)
- Tactically define how the business is going to get there (guidelines and guiding principles)
- Identify and execute on the resulting projects

IV. ADDITIONAL THOUGHTS ON INFRASTRUCTURE

Since infrastructure is the foundation for this strategy I think it warrants additional elaboration and discussion. Please read these passages if you have any reservations at all about the importance of infrastructure investments.

A. Critical Factors

These are the critical factors to keep in mind regarding infrastructure:
- Identify and select the best short-term investments to solve pressing business needs without sacrificing long-term flexibility in architecture.
- Establish a long-term plan to extend a common set of infrastructure principles and standards to the company's enterprise architecture.
- Develop a prioritized list of projects with timelines to implement the elements of the strategic plan.
- Create a strategic plan that will guide both short-term tactical activities and long-term strategic initiatives.
- Provide budgetary quotes for recommended tactical activities and strategies.

B. Philosophy

Many SMBs balk at spending money on infrastructure. There are many reasons for this hesitation but the primary reason seems to be that this spending is presented to the business leader as an optional expenditure. I would like to submit that this is not an optional investment but should be considered as a cost of doing business. Here is why.

Philosophically, the base layer strategy will not differ substantially from any other SMB. It is common in business to feel that each individual business is unique but there are startling similarities across all businesses particularly at the infrastructure level. All small businesses need basically the same things. They need computing power and communications capability. Each must have this functionality to operate.

It is important to note that technology and technology solutions, while still healthy investments, are now less costly and more readily available than ever before. Technology infrastructure has almost become a "me too" proposition. It is rare for any company to gain a competitive advantage or differentiate itself in the marketplace by its use of technology infrastructure. A solid and reliable infrastructure in many SMBs is now achievable and has become somewhat of a commodity in the technology arena.

A properly engineered and maintained infrastructure that employs industrial strength hardware and software solutions from industry leaders also results in lower total cost of ownership, provides greater stability, and is more scalable than an infrastructure that does not adhere to these design philosophies. An underpowered, under-designed, nonstandard infrastructure may cost less initially but the amount of time and effort that an IS staff must spend addressing operational issues and maintaining an inferior infrastructure quickly elevates the cost well beyond the initial savings.

The business gets what it pays for. This rule applies when building a technology infrastructure. The use of low-cost components and inferior technologies no doubt saves money in the short run. However, independent studies and industry experience have consistently demonstrated that this practice costs a business far more than any initial savings. The expense of the daily care and feeding of many low-cost solutions quickly exceeds the money saved. As an example, deploying a used server to host a mission-critical application will provide short-term savings in hardware costs. However, even one brief avoidable failure of the server hardware will exceed the cost saved in deploying uncertified used hardware.

C. Additional Guiding Principles

- **Name brands**

    As previously mentioned, name-brand industry leading hardware should be selected when purchasing servers, switches, routers, and other equipment. Use leading hardware vendors for servers and for network components. For desktop hardware deploy only top-tier PCs. These recommendations are based on mean time between failure, total cost of ownership, the availability of support, and ease of finding technicians or engineers familiar with the equipment. It is also some of the most common equipment used in business today which makes interfacing with clients less complex.

- **Industry leaders**

    Deploy name-brand industry leading software and avoid bleeding edge software, freeware and other inexpensive solutions. Currently this includes Microsoft Windows operating systems on servers and desktops. UNIX and supported forms of Linux are also recommended for certain applications. SQL and Oracle are the only two options that should be considered for enterprise database requirements. The business gets what it pays for and the business can't build a world-class infrastructure on second-tier technology.

- **Scalability**

    Among other criteria, all solutions should be chosen based on their ability to scale. Most businesses are going to grow and the technology put in place needs to grow along with them. Staying with industry leading technology will normally accomplish this goal for the business but always consider a product's growth potential before purchase. Building a network from the inside out will enable the business to push older technologies to the periphery as they approach the end of their life cycles and increase the overall return on investment.

D. Current Industry Trends

- **Infrastructure as a Commodity**

    Over the years, professionals in the IS industry have implemented and retooled numerous technology platforms. The challenges are generally not unique and the solutions have become fairly ubiquitous across all industries. For example, the way networks are designed and implemented is no longer a secret and provides little if any competitive advantage. The network needs to be robust enough to serve the computing needs and scalable enough to warrant little attention or generate little support expense.

- **Outsourcing**

    The trend with many SMBs is strategic outsourcing. This is not to be confused with the wholesale outsourcing of the mid- to late nineties. This strategy parses out layers of the technology infrastructure that are now considered commodities or utilities. These are components that do not deliver any competitive advantage by keeping them in-house and, in reality, drain resources that can be focused on customer activities that have greater impact. Again, independent integrators are always preferable to specific hardware vendors. Make sure the integrators have no overriding commitments to specific vendors.

- **Timing the Moves**

    No matter what the business buys or how well the IS department maintains it, the technology gets old. Some technology life cycles are measured in months and not years. Accounting practices now retire many technology assets in three years instead of the traditional five or seven years. The key to maximizing the value is determining how the business can reuse and when to retire the resource and move on to a new technology.

E. Summary of Additional Thoughts on Infrastructure

The IS department can better achieve the vision outlined in this book by following these guiding principles. In order to build and maintain reliable and scalable infrastructure, it requires knowledgeable industry partners, careful planning, dedicated time, and serious investments in industry standard solutions. Building a solid technology infrastructure is not a single event but a journey that requires continuous attention and investment to maintain a healthy foundation on which to grow the business. The business doesn't need to be on the bleeding edge but it does need to implement solutions that are battle tested and follow generally accepted design standards.

Overcoming Growth Barrier 1   Chapter 4
Business Layer and the Individual

1. *Hackers generally shun structure and methodology.*

2. *The skill sets that got you here may take you no further.*

3. *Determine what new skill sets will be needed by technology layer.*

4. *Management themselves may not be able to navigate the changes. Old habits die hard.*

5. *Develop the department messages and market them.*

6. *Don't overlook the personnel component of strategy and tactics.*

I. INTRODUCTION

This is the third component of the business layer approach and consists of management of the individual in support of the strategy and the tactics.

II. BUSINESS LAYER AND THE INDIVIDUAL

A. The Individual

It is obviously necessary to reevaluate the composition of the IS department personnel. The skills that got the company to this point are not applicable to breaking through this barrier. The technicians or hackers that currently comprise the majority of the IS department will neither realize nor embrace the new approaches required to move forward. All IS leadership may not embrace this change either. The IS department will have to move from being technology generalists to business and technology specialists and they may not have the requisite specialized skill sets.

B. The Staff

Let's look first at what is needed. Under the above scenario, the business will need within the IS department:

- **In infrastructure for managing projects and activities**

  For the infrastructure, the IS department will need a technical relationship manager skill set to manage the vision, direction, vendors, solutions, projects, consultants, and relationships. The IS department will need one or more of these relationship management employees. The skill set depends on an understanding of technology but not the ability to dabble with it. It requires excellent organization and communication skills. It requires an understanding of vendor relationship management. It requires knowledge of the business and the internal and external business processes. This position requires a combination of strategic and tactical skill sets. The IS department may not have even one of these individuals on the existing staff.

- **In back office systems**

  For the back office, the IS department will need a system analyst skill set to understand, coordinate, document, support, design, select, manage, and integrate the various application software and hardware system solutions. The IS department will need one or more of these system analyst employees. As with infrastructure, the skill set depends on an understanding of technology but not the ability to dabble with it. It requires excellent organization and communication skills. It requires an understanding of vendor relationship management. Again, business understanding and a process approach are paramount. This position requires a combination of strategic and tactical skill sets. The IS department may not have even one of these individuals on the existing staff.

- **In customer facing systems**

  The IS department will need a creative technical skill set to research, design, develop, project manage, and support customer solutions. The skill sets here are mostly tactical. They require an excellent technical understanding and more than a little creativity. The hacker mentality is important here but needs to be tempered with market awareness and the ability to evaluate and select software solutions. Here is where some of the existing IS staff may shine. If the business is able to retain any of the existing staff it will be in this area.

From an IS staff member perspective, one of the most distressing facts about realigning the IS department with a new strategy is that many of the existing personnel will not negotiate the changes. As with strategy and tactics that must change as the business changes, so must the personnel. Please remember that most of the hackers do not believe in structure and methodology and do believe that processes—like project management—are unnecessary bureaucracy. These are very creative people and they see their jobs as art. The business is trying to make their job a science. The business should expect an incredible amount of backlash from the IS team but changes must be made.

These are very difficult times because most of the department's time is spent on daily maintenance and support. Since the IS department is people-dependent and not process- or documentation-dependent, the business leadership risks business disruption when changes are made. The IS department will also have difficulty squeezing out time for any new projects and any strategic exercises. No one should expect that these transitions will be easy. Before it makes any changes the business might consider hiring a documentation specialist and initiating a serious documentation effort to work through gathering and improving on the documentation.

Before making personnel changes attempt to perform an in-depth staff analysis looking for several key factors that may enable the business to keep an employee instead of releasing them. The goal is to retain the IS intellectual capital where at all possible. Look for:

- an open-minded and education hungry attitude
- background, education, and training in larger organizations
- ability to communicate well verbally and in writing
- open to change and flexible in work habits
- a business focus and a business understanding

It is important to make as many changes as possible at one time. It is difficult to maintain morale during continued and constant staff reductions and cutbacks.

C. The Management

IS management will also be severely challenged. This is not to say that they have not contributed to the success of the organization and been responsible for bringing the business this far. Please remember that this failure point is preordained and no one should be held responsible or punished. The concept of a no-fault divorce is relevant. The hard facts are that the skills that got the business to this point are of little use in the next evolution of the business. Smaller company employees tend to stay smaller company employees. Few make the transition. It might be part of their career path to move from one startup organization to another. The business now has some tough choices. Many SMBs continue to flounder, and ultimately may fail, because the IS leadership did not adapt and the business leadership refused to make the necessary changes. In most cases the skills that the IS management brought to the table are technical and not strategic. These managers seldom possess strategic skills. At this juncture, IS management must go through a sizable strategic transition and they may not want to or be able to do it. It is a difficult thing to acknowledge and even tougher to deal with.

D. Messages

The IS team needs to have a vision and a clear direction. I have extracted the messages below that I have used in real-life situations. They are fairly universal and will doubtless come in handy. The business and IS leadership will need to carry these to the remaining IS team members. The message needs to be consistent and relentless. This is what the business should expect.

- **State of the department**

  We are a strong technical team. We are creative and innovative. We are great at quick, creative problem solving. However, our solutions are not always robust and industrial strength. Many seem to need tweaking and constant maintenance. We have not marketed ourselves or our services. We have become informal and relaxed with no self-imposed standards. There is not enough discipline and no sense of urgency. While our company may not be spending enough on technology, this must change. We can facilitate this change by a focus on return on investment, the utility approach, and developing business cases for spending. We have not been rigid enough in scheduling and meeting deadlines.

- **Service**

  We must remember that we have two sets of clients or customers—external and internal. We want to be a service organization so we must first think about servicing our users and aligning our activities to support the business. We are not a technology organization but a service organization. We need to be proactive in our services.

- **Marketing**

  We must market our services. We must change the current negative perceptions about ourselves and our services. We will produce capability statements that adequately describe what we can do and how we can do it. We will also make it easy to work with us. We will provide proactive sales support since sales drive the company and provide us with our compensation. We will develop an aggressive marketing plan to win over our users.

- **Day to day we will raise the bar**

  We must maintain a sense of urgency. Every interaction with the user community is an opportunity to perform. We will be cheerful, considerate, enthusiastic, and helpful in our interactions. We will strive to make measurable progress every day. We will track and measure what we do. We will develop our own scorecards. We will solve daily problems with solutions that position us for long-term growth.

- **Educate**

  We will explain what it is that we do and how long it takes. We will educate our users about technology and demystify what we do. We will develop and provide a technology tip of the week feature that will reduce our overall corporate training costs.

- **Utility approach**

  Our basic technology infrastructure services (layers one and two) need to be viewed as utilities. They will work without failure and should be taken for granted because they are so reliable. We will identify the utility portion of our infrastructure and strive to make these like utilities.

- **Production approach**

    We will take a production mentality and approach to running our technology and develop schedules and automated controls. We will formalize our processes, procedures, standards, and guidelines. We will attempt to formalize, standardize, document, and put applications into production.

- **Software development**

    We will emphasize buying before building software due to the size of staff and speed of delivery. We need to formalize the software selection process by taking the following approaches:
    - Use data flow diagrams, requirements, and design documents
    - Conduct white board sessions
    - Assure that no project will last more than ninety days
    - Use phased implementation so we deliver early and often
    - Use standard tools and approaches with a web-based or browser approach

- **Kinds of work we will do in IS (top or customer layer)**

    It is of the utmost importance that we provide existing client support and support sales and opportunity prospecting. We will conduct structured research and development within relevant technology spheres. We will encourage and solicit technical questions and discussions. Specifically, we will:
    - Support existing clients
        - Provide initial service definition
        - Provide initial configuration and setup
        - Conduct fine-tuning of ongoing support processes
        - Fix problems
    - Provide software selection and integration
        - Gather business requirements
        - Perform package evaluations
        - Perform package selections
        - Assist where needed in package installations

III. SUMMARY

This business layer strategy is designed to enable the business to break through the first real IS barrier and move to the next growth level. It requires strict coordination of the strategy, the tactics, and the management of the individuals.

Growth Level 2

> **WISDOM to work by:**
>
> 1. One size does not fit all. No single strategy and no strategy enactment works forever.
> 2. The business and the IS department will surely reach another barrier.
> 3. The business layer strategy may have neglected solutions that will grow and scale with the business.
> 4. Again, the things the business has done to get them here are the things that begin to work against them.

I. INTRODUCTION

If the business was fortunate enough to initiate the business layer strategy, or somehow otherwise manage to get past the first growth barrier, it will ultimately hit the second. At this point in the company history the business layer model or whatever other solution was chosen will begin to falter. The business leadership may not, at first, recognize this as the source of the discomfort or identify the end of the business layer strategy's usefulness as the culprit. By now, if experiences are normal, the business has added many employees and probably many more products and services. It has increased the number of technology solutions and business applications. The business has increased in both size and complexity. The customer base has increased as well and with that the clamoring for improved products or services. Despite the best efforts and a focus on these concerns, the technology solutions have begun to have issues of scalability and connectivity. The business has grown to the point where the various technology layers, while stable, are impediments to growth. The office systems are being taxed to the point of distraction. The IS vendor's products, both software and hardware, may have reached the end of their life cycles. The accounting package doesn't provide the complex reporting and financial data that is now needed. The telephone system lacks the larger company functions and features being demanded. The network, rather than being an enabler, prevents the business from working with new clients. The business may consider acquiring other companies to increase revenue or supplement product lines. These acquisitions are not possible due to the inability of the back office solutions to scale and network. The technology solutions, while not point solutions, are not broad enough to cover new business possibilities and new business opportunities.

To summarize, the strategic approach using the business layer model got the business to this point but the solutions are no longer working. The solutions that were chosen were right at the time but now prevent leadership from keeping up with the business changes. The basic problem is that the technology solutions are not broad enough or strategic enough. There is a world of growth possibilities that the business cannot embrace because the solution set is too narrow. The business is looking to the IS department to bail the business out but they are not responding. The skill sets and strengths that got the business through the first barrier are not robust enough to get it through the next barrier. Another IT barrier will be reached and the business is, quite naturally, stymied again.

II. STRATEGY

From a strategic perspective, the business layer approach as a strategy will have been effective. The approach has some built-in shortcomings because the business vision and the associated technology budget that supported it were naturally limited in scope. Now that the business has grown and expanded the technology strategy and the technology budget must be expanded as well. Again, this barrier will naturally vary by industry, market, or company but the event will inevitably occur. The current barrier is linked to the failure of the business and IS to recognize their own strategic drivers and to identify the right technologies to deploy to accommodate growth. The business does not know which technologies are important to grow the business, where the technology dollars should be invested, or how much to invest. The IS department lacks an enterprise focus and a proper structure for selecting technologies. The business layer approach is not sophisticated enough to provide the proper view of the business. Again, the business could only spend based on what could be afforded at the time.

III. TACTICS

There are negative business symptoms that will be experienced. The business has gotten through the last hurdle. The strategy and tactics were working so well that it became an ingrained process and the business is now surprised when the IS department begins to falter again. Whether in a slow- or fast-paced growth phase, the business does have more dollars to spend as a result of increased revenues. There is greater internal competition for the dollars from various departments (sales, marketing, business development) while the business is struggling to put reasonable limits on what products or services it needs to provide. Business leadership knows they can't be all things to all customers. Market share is steady and growing consisting of, most likely, a couple of large and numerous small clients. Business leadership has identified the largest competitors but don't know their secrets. The business leadership has the uneasy feeling that the competitors' technologies and approaches are the keys to their dominance in the marketplace. The business realizes that growth and untapped markets are available but as yet it doesn't know how to exploit them. The business is growing but it has reached a barrier it can't seem to surmount and business leadership has the feeling that it can't get there from here.

The business has reached hurdle 2. It is characterized primarily by the business leadership knowing they have specific technology hurdles and impediments but they don't know what technology solutions to deploy or embrace. Most projects fail or are failing, and when successful provide little to no practical value. Business leadership has the strong feeling that the IS department is doing the wrong projects and the wrong things. The business leadership knows they have spent too little on technology or invested in the wrong technologies. The IS group appears to have become a group of non-responsive order takers. There is no technology vision. There appears to be no sense of urgency within the IS department. While the IS investment continues to grow the return on investment is diminishing. The IS department is starting to experience employee turnover in both management and staff.

IV. THE INDIVIDUAL

There are negative IS symptoms that will be experienced. The IS department is again reactive, not proactive, and appears to have slipped back to the old ways. The IS department is considered simply order takers and not true business partners. IS leadership had become excluded from management meetings and the business decision-making process. There are some technology solutions that are scaling well but many are not. IS is not impacting the business in a positive way and the department members are beginning to question their roles in the organization. The business conducts projects without IS participation. Some of these projects are even technology-centric.

The IS department is competing for investment dollars but doesn't know how to ask or what to ask for...other than one-off or point solutions. IS again lacks vision. The IS department spends a lot of time on projects that are never completed or have lost relevance to the business. The IS department doesn't know how to deal with these setbacks. Daily the IS department is asked to build a lot of simple one-off solutions. They feel they are dictated technology solutions and not asked to solve business problems. The business sees IS as out of touch and only marginally relevant. The business looks for ways to work around IS and not with them. There is more money being spent within the IS budget but fewer results are being delivered. There is no longer a viable IS strategy. Documentation and training have slipped and user service and support has again become a major issue.

V. SUMMARY

Once again the IS department is an impediment to the business and not an asset. In the defined business cycle this is not an unusual occurrence. This is a normal and natural outcome of business growth. It is simple cause and effect. The business layer approach is sound and effective but it will only take the business so far. The strategy has outlived its usefulness. It does provide a very good foundation on which to build and the business will not have to totally scrap all solutions and start over. The IS department now needs a technology-centric focus and a fresh look at the business. The business now needs to look at selective technology investments that they previously could not afford. The business was limited in technology choices by budgetary restraints. The business is now faced with selective expansion and/or replacement of prior technology solutions with more enterprise-wide, robust solutions that they previously could not afford to deploy. The IS department needs to go about addressing technology in a completely different way.

For this section of the book, describing the business model approach to strategy, I will use a business example. While describing the strategic process in detail can be effective, the use of examples provides a much more effective way to describe this strategic exercise. The example I will use is a sanitized version of a strategy I prepared for a previous employer. The company no longer exists and the versions I am using are generalized enough to distance us from the real-life example and generic enough that we will be able to use the relevant concepts. The business is that of a mail-order medical supplier of medical products that treat long-term diseases like diabetes or incontinence. The details and vagaries of that business can be found in the examples used below.

Business Model Strategy

WISDOM to work by:

1. *Time to embrace a totally technology focused strategy.*

2. *An effective IT strategy matches the business strategy, if available, or has general applicability based on the overt business activities.*

3. *It all starts with the business model.*

4. *Layer in the technology models:*
    a. *The software view*
    b. *The hardware view*
    c. *The network view*

5. *Mapping the technology models to the business model produces strategic areas of focus.*

6. *The IS strategy will use the strategic areas of focus to leverage the right technologies and remove technology impediments.*

7. *Know your strategic drivers. What makes your situation different?*

I. INTRODUCTION

Please reference appendices 6.1 (Business Model Strategy) and 6.2 (Business Model Tactics) which summarize the recommended approach. This is the approach to follow to again remove IS and technology from being a business impediment. At this point in the company history the business needs to embrace a totally technology focused strategy. This will be a very difficult strategy for the business to embrace without having some business members who are very strong in technology. To remedy this situation the business should either use outside consulting resources or hire additional strategic IS leadership to take control. It will take a knowledgeable technology leader to make this work. Following those steps, the business can identify the direction the technology should take and identify specific technologies and projects to execute. This strategic approach will get the business through the next major barrier. It is more formal and time-consuming. The strategic keys to success will be the tools and techniques found here to structure this exercise.

II. STRATEGY

A. Definitions

The following set of strategic exercises requires an agreement on both philosophy and terminology. The business leadership needs to assist the IS leadership in analyzing the business from a technology perspective and selecting the technologies that will enable the business to realize unrestrained growth. Some clarity on terminology is required at this point in time as well. I recommend the following definitions:

- **Business strategies** - These define what the business is going to do at a high level to grow and prosper. This includes products, services, markets, financial and manpower goals and objectives, and any other stated directives.
- **IS strategic areas of focus** - These are a response to the stated business strategy or business needs. It is a method of identifying and grouping the required technologies in a cohesive and unified way in order to solve enterprise-wide requirements. Examples of IS strategic areas of focus could include the following:
  - Document management
  - Customer relationship management
  - Common systems
- **Individual IS strategic areas of focus** - These are enacted through execution of a set of IS-related projects. These projects fit together from both a technology and business process flow perspective to support the IS strategy. Examples include a document management strategy comprised of the following:
  - Standardized document project
  - Print engine project
  - Fax server project
  - Unified messaging project

B. The Business Model

As with any successful exercise, and similar to the business layer model, before the business can map where it is going it needs to know where it is today. This strategy uses a more sophisticated approach yet one based on some fairly simplistic modeling. It requires that the business develop business models and technology models to describe the current state. Then, using other strategic tools, the business can chart a new direction.

The business model describes how the business works from a macro level. It should be a one- to two-page document that basically shows how the product or service provided by the business is delivered. I find it best depicted in the form of a flowchart. Please refer to the sample business model provided as appendix 6.3. The business model is not a detailed document but rather shows the primary high-level business processes. The business will then need to develop the sub-processes beneath each of the major business processes. I have included a sample as appendix 6.4. The customer interaction with the business to get products and services follows a set repeatable pattern. While it obviously differs from business to business, it is usually a very simple process flow. This process generally begins with a sale or order and proceeds through the internal business processes culminating in order fulfillment for the customer and revenue to the business. The ultimate use of this business model is to define and document a description of the core business processes with accompanying business parameters.

The business model is the starting point and the basis for this strategic exercise. It defines and documents the core business processes that are basically required to conduct the business. It provides a process view of the business. It is a high-level view which can be used to view the business in discreet individual or process segments.

C. The Technology Model

The technology model is a little more complex and has several uses. It is a multi-page document (views) showing how IS has constructed the various technology systems in support of the business system. A technology model lists the hardware, software (including database), and network components assembled in support of the business. The technology model defines the service delivery configuration in generic process terms and in specific hardware, software, and network terms.

D. Technology Model Views

An example of a set of technology views follows.

1. View 1 – Software and Database View

The software view shows the software and applications that are currently used to support the business model processes. Like the business model it is easiest to depict in a flowchart form. Please reference appendix 6.5 for an example. The attachment lists the various software solutions that have been deployed to support the business model. If the business has not used the business layer approach or some other rigid methodology, this view will most likely be a real mess. The IS department will have bought or built function-ality by piecing the entire thing together. The business may be using as little as 10 percent of a purchased package's functionality or as much as 90 percent. The business will have several solutions from several vendors with internally developed or vendor-supplied inter-faces. These solutions were working well at the time they were selected and implemented. They provided functionality leaps that were not present before. Now, however, they may have become impediments to growth. Most applications will be using flat files, MS Excel files, MS Access databases and, if the business is fortunate, a few SQL databases.

The ultimate purpose of this exercise is to examine the software and database port-folio and identify strengths, weaknesses, and opportunities. In addition to the flowchart view, the business will need to develop a spreadsheet listing the individual components of the software suite. On the sheet there should be columns for the database or data structures being used and the additional software characteristics listed below. At a minimum track the following:
  - Software limitations
  - Reporting tools
  - Scalability of the application

- Functionality strengths and weaknesses
- Positive and negative features
- Reliability of the system
- The age and maturity of the system
- Whether the software was purchased or developed
- Acceptance by user community and general reputation of the system
- Timings and responsiveness
- Numerical or quantitative limitations
- Whether or not the application is web enabled
- Modularity of construction
- Whether the application is ultimately going to be kept or replaced

If the IS department is using any database other than industry leaders like Oracle or MS SQL server, they should plan for a change. While there are other and possibly better databases, these are the industry leaders and market share dictates the players. Using another database will cause the IS department to have trouble with everything from finding qualified database administrators to getting new functionality and new releases.

2. View 2 – Hardware/Platform View

The hardware or platform view will simply list the existing hardware configuration. It is a given that this will not be an optimal configuration and that there will be an odd mix of hardware and vendors. It is best depicted in a network diagram form that should relate closely to the software and business model views. Please reference appendix 6.6 for a sample hardware/platform view. By the way, deploying four to eight different platforms is not uncommon. This picture is usually more complex than the business first imagines despite previous efforts to standardize.

In addition to the hardware/platform diagram, develop some accompanying narrative. Specifically, develop statements about each component on the diagram. These statements should speak to the same issues identified in the software/database view. Please refer to those bullet points above. If the business has used the business layer approach in earlier growth stages, it is well-positioned to evaluate the technology areas and plan for growth. Here are some sample statements for guidance.

- **Sample statement 1 - NT servers** - The NT servers are modular and can be grown and configured in various ways. There are no known limiting factors.
- **Sample statement 2 - Legacy host processors** - The legacy host processors are also a modular solution that can be grown or clustered together in various ways. We are limited by the age of the solution and the limited tool sets available.
- **Sample statement 3 - Telephony** - The telephony solution is not only limited strictly by size but also by features and functions provided. We lack the following features (provide list).

3. View 3 – Network View

This third technology model will show the LAN, WAN, and Internet connectivity components. It should also be depicted in a network diagram view and be easy to relate to previously developed views. These last two views are much more specific in terms of defining the specific technology components and model numbers. This view is commonly done in all IS organizations and should be constantly kept current and made available for this kind of exercise. Since a network diagram is fairly universal, I have not included a sample.

Using the network diagram view develop statements about each component on the diagram. These statements should speak to the same issues identified in the software/database view. Please refer to those bullet points above. Evaluate the limitations and growth opportunities in each of the areas. If the business has used the business layer approach in earlier growth stages, it is well-positioned to evaluate the technology areas and plan for growth. Here are some sample statements for guidance.

- **Sample statement 1 - Switches and routers** - These are modular components and can be grown and configured in various ways. There are no limiting factors.
- **Sample statement 2 - LAN** - We have been using dumb routers instead of intelligent switches and we need to replace these or we cannot proactively monitor our network.
- **Sample statement 3 - Connectivity** - We have issues with our current software that links the home office to the warehouse. The connection is unreliable and hard to troubleshoot. We need to replace it.

E. The Technology Model Summary

The business now has a concise picture of where the business and the supporting technology reside today. Now let's see where it should go.

F. The Business Strategy

1. Confirm the Business Model

As with the business layer approach, the business model approach requires the business to conduct a strategic exercise to either confirm the business model or make modifications to it. If the business model is confirmed as correct and will not change, the challenge is to focus on the enabling technologies that will remove the barriers to growth. If there are changes to the business model, based on new products or services or other process changes, then the business model needs to be redrawn before proceeding. The business model is the essence of the business model strategy.

2. Document Technology Impediments to Growth

Next compile in a single document all of the technology impediments to growth. This is accomplished by assembling all of the flows and narratives from the three technology models and collating them into a single comprehensive document. From this narrative we can draw general conclusions and develop a comprehensive document. The IS strategy will be geared toward enabling growth and progress by removing these technology impediments.

3. **Develop the New Technology Vision**

Based on the current state of the business and the existing IS solutions, tempered and modified by any new business strategy, the next step is to develop an IS technology vision that addresses the problems with and shortcomings of technology. This should be in the form of a narrative and accompanying model views. Take each of the technology model views and reconstruct them using generic components labeled to reflect the grouping of functionalities that you need. I have attached a sample software technology vision as appendix 6.7. Please refer to it. These generic components will become specific strategic components as a result of the next series of exercises. If these can be properly addressed the impediments to business growth can be removed. By focusing on the business and technology models and the deltas or opportunities between the two, we can identify the technologies that are important to the business. We can identify the strategic areas of technology focus that will allow the business to grow. This exercise will result in a period of time where the technology can actually drive the business. This is a very powerful exercise!

G. IS Strategy Summary

We are now ready to develop the strategy. The strategy will be expressed as a set of broad strategic areas of focus. The IS strategy is based on an alignment of the needs of the business with the application and deployment of the IS resources to satisfy those needs. The IS strategy is developed as a convenient way to address all of the pressing needs of the business in broader focused initiatives and assure that common business problems across product groupings are resolved with consistency and forethought.

When we discuss IS strategies remember that we are talking about the following: an IS strategy is a convenient way to organize and address a large number of initiative-related projects that build into a composite strategy.

The scope of the IS strategy enables proper sequencing and execution of projects, as well as building on previous projects. It also enables the business to address other areas, like documentation and training, along with the requisite technology acquisition.

The primary benefit of an IS strategy is the single vision with a defined path describing how to get there. The best way to accomplish results using business strategies is through creation and support of business strategy teams. I will define these teams later.

H. Strategic Areas of Focus

The IS strategy can now be defined as a set of broad strategic areas of focus by using the technology vision models we have developed. With the models and a straightforward process approach, the business can define the strategic areas where the IS department should be focused. I believe there is a universality of business processes and broad strategies that are common among various businesses. I am referring to the need to do things like manage documents and handle customer calls. These technologies can be identified strategically and applied to the various high-level business processes. Based on what the business is trying to accomplish, the business needs to identify those technologies and solutions that will bring the greatest functionality and effectiveness to the business.

As an example, one of the requirements of the mail-order medical supply business was to obtain written permission from both the doctor and the patient before shipping product. This was originally being done through snail mail and paper fax. It was a repetitive, time-consuming, and inefficient operation. Papers were mailed to the patient and had to be signed and returned. It took repetitive mailings to secure the appropriate signature. Papers were faxed to the doctor's office and were supposed to be signed and returned. This was also a repetitive process that took several attempts before it could be successful. The result was paper documents everywhere and floor space consumed in vast quantities. By making the observation that the business was paperbound, and possessing a basic knowledge of imaging and other document handling technologies, it was not much of a leap to see that document management had to be both an inhibitor to the business and necessarily a strategic area of focus. With this observational leap, the strategic area of focus could be defined, scoped out, and turned into a series of projects that would build the vision into a reality.

The following uses the mail-order medical supply business as an example and shows examples of how the strategic area of focus can be built out into a legitimate strategy. We were able to identify several strategies that, if realized, would position the business for incredible growth and profitability. Two of these will serve as an example. They are as follows:

- Document Management
- Call Management

Example 1 – Document Management Strategy

Document Management Business Strategy Summary

- **Definition** - All systems (hardware and software) required to automate document handling requirements that are needed to carry out the business.
- **Vision** - To implement an enterprise-wide, centralized document handling system with access from any desktop connected to the corporate network.
- **Benefits** - Increase agent productivity by eliminating the need to walk to fax machines or do department printing. Increase agent productivity through electronic storage and retrieval of documents. Minimize the handling of paper documents. Minimize compliance risks that could be created through errors during transcribing and handling of documents.
- **Risks** - Rapid acquisitions and associated integration activity may limit resources available for this development initiative.
- **Constraints** - Time to execute the projects.

- **Assumptions** - Necessary capital will be made available. Necessary staffing with appropriate skill sets will be available. This is a development project and will share its allocated development human resources with other development activities. Solutions will be scaled down to match revenue models and projections. Solutions will scale up with the growth of the organization. Tools will be purchased to centrally manage the solution(s). A high-speed, high-bandwidth, self-healing, and redundant wide area network is in place. Solutions include faxing, scanning, and electronic storage and retrieval.
- **Inclusions**
    - ○ **Activities** - Document printing, document faxing, document imaging, document storage, document retrieval, document bar coding, and document handling.
    - ○ **Documents** - Claims, invoices, and any other printed, faxed, or electronic documents.
- **Governing parameters** - Provide the appropriate document at the appropriate time and at the least overall cost to the organization.
- **Description of Technologies**
    - ○ **Document Imaging, Storage, and Retrieval** - Document imaging involves scanning the paper documents and storing the image electronically. These documents are indexed in such a way that agents can retrieve and display these images across the network on desktop devices.
    - ○ **Document Bar Coding** - Document bar coding involves printing specific data fields translated into bar codes. Documents are then exchanged with customers, physicians, and insurers. When returned, these documents are scanned and the bar code is electronically read. This eliminates manual keying of these data fields.

IS recommends the following document management strategy and recommends that the business develop the required capability and realize the vision through a series of projects that standardize and centralize all document handling functions. The business should execute the following projects:

- **Standardize Documents** - Develop a standard way to store and retrieve documents regardless of the delivery vehicle.
- **Document Printing** - Centralize and standardize document printing. Reduce corporate printing costs by at least 10 percent.
- **Document Imaging, Storage, and Retrieval** - Centralize and image appropriate documents. Provide electronic storage and retrieval of document images. Eliminate the document filing room. Eliminate manual document searching and retrieval.
- **Document Bar Coding** - Deploy bar code printing and scanning of appropriate data fields with the goal of reducing or eliminating excessive document handling and keying of data. Reduce cost of document handling and keying of data fields by at least 10 percent.
- **Document Faxing** - Centralize electronic, individual and mass faxing, or eliminate paper faxing where possible. Reduce paper faxing by 100 percent.

- **Document Emailing** - Centralize and standardize emailed documents.
- **Electronic Interfaces** - Centralize and standardize handling of electronic files and interfaces.

Example 2 – Call Management Strategy

Call Management Business Strategy Summary

- **Definition** - All systems (hardware and software) required to process inbound and outbound telephone calls. The systems manage all aspects (from marketing to distribution) of our business.
- **Vision** - To build a world-class call center environment utilizing industry standard best practices and technology.
- **Benefit** - Increase inbound and outbound call handling efficiency thereby reducing the number of agents required. Enable seamless integration of the small work group concept while achieving cost savings associated with large call centers. Increase customer intimacy through a near one-to-one relationship.
- **Risks** - Limited experience within the business with call center operations management. Rapid acquisitions and associated integration activity may limit resources available for this development initiative.
- **Constraints** - All calls must be answered and processed through human voice interaction.
- **Assumptions** - Necessary capital will be made available. Necessary staffing with appropriate skill sets will be available. This is a development project and will share its allocated development human resources with other development activities. Solutions will be scaled down to match revenue models and projections. Solutions will scale up with the growth of the organization. Tools will be purchased to centrally manage the solutions. Advanced call handling technology will be added.
- **Detailed Vision**
    - ○ **Inputs** - Inputs will be daily transactional work queues developed from existing customer databases. The queues will be built when action is required.
    - ○ **Processing** - Processing focuses on the telephone interaction between customers and agents. Inbound and outbound calls flow through the main telephone system and one or more of the functional technologies.
    - ○ **Outputs** - Outputs will include daily tangible results consisting of new customers, completed documentation, and reorders.
- **Governing Parameters** - The governing parameter is to always have a successful interaction between the customer and the agent. This success is measured by:
    - ○ **Customer Contacting Company** - Customer contact rate should approach 100 percent during published business hours. Provide 100 percent rollover to voice mail during non-business hours. All previously gathered customer information will be available to the agent. All information will be made available with minimal searching and screen sifting. Provide shortened agent training time due to ease of use.

  ○ **Company Contacting Customer**
  Company contact rate should be 100 percent for a live agent and a live customer or answering machine. All previously gathered customer information will be made available to the agent. All information will be made available with minimal searching and screen sifting. Calls will be made at the appropriate time in the customer cycle. Calls should not be made too early or too late. Eliminate repetitive attempts to make customer contact. Provide shortened agent training time due to ease of use.

- **Description of Technologies**
  ○ **ACD Functionality** - Automatic Call Distribution (ACD) serves as a traffic cop for telephone calls. It enables calls to be handled more efficiently and effectively by sending calls to the appropriate agent based on programmable factors. ACD allows for call receiving, routing, stacking, messaging, and connecting. It often gathers the data used in computer telephony interface (CTI) applications. It greatly increases the chances that the customer will speak to the appropriate agent and have a successful call experience.
  ○ **Predictive Dialer Functionality** - Predictive Dialers serve as screening agents. They screen out all calls that will not result in an agent speaking directly to a customer. They screen out all busy signals, disconnected telephones, unanswered phones, and answering machines. Predictive Dialers also serve as call regulators. They regulate the speed of outbound dialing in an attempt to keep all agents talking and not have a customer available without an agent to talk to them. This is done by sophisticated pacing algorithms that calculate a calling pace based on the number of available agents, the average number of telephone numbers being dialed to get a customer on the phone, the average talk time of the agents, and the number of outbound lines available to dial through.
  ○ **CTI Functionality** - Computer Telephony Integration (CTI) brings together voice and data technologies to improve agent productivity. It usually involves interrogating data from an inbound call to make queries against databases over a local area network. The inbound call data may come from capturing the originating telephone number, by asking the caller to press keypad numbers, or by voice recognition. The databases are used to make decisions about the caller and to present appropriate information about the caller to the agent.

IS management recommends the following call management strategy: develop the required capability and realize the vision through a series of projects that add the appropriate technology. Conduct the following projects:
- Call center training and PBX software upgrade
- ACD training and rollout
- Report training and rollout
- Dialer training and rollout
- Voice mail training and rollout
- Voice-over-IP training and rollout
- Advanced ACD and CTI training and rollout

III. STRATEGIC DRIVERS

The business should now be able to identify four to six strategic areas of focus. Any more or less and the business will most likely not be focusing on the right things. Given success in defining the strategic areas of focus (defines the what), the business should now focus on the strategic drivers (defines the how). These are guiding principles or drivers that must be used during the tactical execution of the projects generated out of the strategy. These drivers are important because they allow IS management to make better technology choices and focus on the factors and considerations that are important and particular to the business.

The IS strategy is the culmination of a series of exercises that encompassed looking across the business organization and identifying those key business processes and technology focus areas that are most critical to making the business and IS a success. Strategic drivers enable the IS leadership to make the right technology choices based on what has been observed to be right for the business. These technology choices are there and facing the business…no matter what the strategic drivers. There are a multitude of ways to select and deploy technologies. The business must have guidelines and ground rules in order to choose wisely.

1. Examples of Strategic Drivers

Using my example of a mail-order medical supply company, we were able to identify our strategic areas of focus as the following:
- Call Center Management
- Document Management

The next strategic exercise consists of examining the strategic areas of focus, factoring in the corporate situation and perspective, and selecting the resulting strategic drivers for the IS organization. It is largely an observational exercise. It consists of conducting a meeting or a series of meetings between the IS management and a business advisory team. It consists of a series of brainstorming sessions that focus on the following areas:

What is the strategy of the company? Have the business executives identified the strategic drivers for the business? Is the business currently customer focused or internally focused? Is the business focused on producing a product or providing a service? How do the business executives approach the customers and the business?

What is the frequency and focus of the "customer touches"? How often does the customer come in contact with the organization? What is the content and message of these contacts? What information or goods and services are exchanged? What is important to the company about these exchanges?

How is the company focused on the industry? Is the company an industry leader or an industry follower? Is the company a trendsetter or a trend follower? Who is the competition and what is known about them? How does the competition differentiate themselves? What are the trends in the industry? What is the focus?

The answers to these questions and the dialogue surrounding these discussions lead to some solid conclusions about the current environment. These answers simply need to be translated into strategic guidelines or strategic factors which must weigh heavily in all technology decisions and all strategic systems development. These become statements of fact that support the business direction and enable the business to structure decisions with fixed criteria. Using our example of a mail-order medical supply business, the strategic drivers might well look like this:

a. **Customer Specific**

 Due to our company focus on customer service, our technology and systems will be flexible enough to enable customization based on the specific needs of our customers. We cannot afford to take a mass production approach because our customers require different solutions based on their particular circumstances. It is expensive to acquire and maintain customers so we must guard them carefully. Our competitors are customizing. In order to be competitive, we must also customize.

b. **Product Focused**

 Since a wide array of products are required to successfully compete in the marketplace, our technology and systems will be full-featured enough to support specific demands of the various product groups. There are distinct groups of customers in our customer community with needs that are different enough to require different product groupings. We must build or buy systems that have a broad range of features and that are not single feature specific. We must build or buy flexible solutions that have a wider range of features than we currently provide or support. We need to focus not only on the current products provided but possible related products as well.

c. **Industry Standards**

 As an IS organization, our technology and selected systems will adhere to industry standards with regard to underlying component technologies and open interfaces. We know we are growing at a rapid rate and that we will face larger integration issues down the road. We must be careful not to select point or one-off solutions that solve narrow specific problems but do not fit into a long-range strategy. We will be cognizant of the need to tie all of our technology and systems together at a later date and that all technology and systems will be required to interact and share information and data. Only through following industry standards can we assure that our decisions today keep our options open for tomorrow.

d. **Tightly Integrated**

 We cannot afford the problems created by disparate systems so our technology and systems will be made to seamlessly integrate among the various selected components. We have a small computer operations capability and we do not have full production monitoring on all shifts. We cannot afford system outages due to integration problems. We do not have the staff to constantly chase and resolve system-related integration problems so we must tightly integrate all systems from the start.

e. Common Systems

We cannot afford to support a wide range of solutions so our technology and systems will be limited to the smallest number of possible solutions with limited duplication of solution sets. The small budget and limited manpower dictate that we narrow the number of deployed solutions. We must look to add functionality and depth of scope to the solutions already deployed and not add like solutions to the mix. This may entail some lost functionality but the support required rises exponentially with the number of solutions deployed.

These strategic drivers and their definitions and explanations should serve as good examples. They should trigger thinking and allow thoughts to coalesce around drivers that will solve current problems and eliminate some of the mistakes made in the past. There is no limit to the number or type of strategic drivers that may be selected but five to six should suffice. The business goal is to assure that these drivers do not conflict and do not leave gaps in the decision-making process. The strategic drivers will not be unique to any single company or any single industry.

IV. BUSINESS MODEL STRATEGY SUMMARY

This strategy works. An effective IT strategy matches the business strategy if it is readily available. If not, the business model strategy has general applicability based on the approach the business is taking and the focus on growth. Mapping the technology models to the business model is the key strategic exercise. Once the SMB identifies the strategic areas of focus and the strategic drivers, it will be poised for action.

Business Model Tactics

1. *Tactics bring the business model strategy to fruition.*

2. *Establish IS strategic teams to own the strategic areas of focus.*

3. *The strategic areas of focus lead to identification of the right project choices.*

4. *Project management becomes the key to tactical success.*

5. *The "Plan, Build, Run" project execution approach works.*

6. *Time tracking is the key to project capacity and project planning. Know how you spend your time.*

7. *Use the IT Council to broker the IS strategic teams.*

8. *Project reporting—keep it simple.*

I. INTRODUCTION

Execution (or tactics) consists of converting IS strategic areas of focus into projects and executing these projects. The strategic exercise is now complete and the business has a blueprint for changing the technology backbone of the company. Execution now becomes the key and the amount of change that will be required should not be underestimated. To successfully execute, the business will have to redirect the IS team and change the way that the business deals with IS. The tactical approach below will get the business through the barrier. I recommend the following sequence of events:

*   Establish IS strategic teams
*   Identify the projects
*   Sequence the projects
*   Execute the projects

II. THE TACTICS

A. Create IS Strategic Teams

As we have learned, developing the IS strategic areas of focus allows the business to develop broad technology focus areas. These will be guided and governed by our strategic drivers. The strategic areas of focus will need to be further broken down into components that will ultimately translate into a series of projects. These projects will need to be owned and executed to enact the strategy. The best method I have found to achieve ownership is through a team effort and something I call the IS strategic teams. These teams are a joint effort between IS and the business created specifically to execute the strategies. IS strategic teams can be tasked with the definition, development, and installation of a series of projects. The team needs to be comprised of members from the following groups:

- Senior business management (VP, directors, managers)
- Affected business groups (leads, supervisors)
- IS technology infrastructure team (engineers)
- IS application development team (software developers)
- Independent external integrators and partners (technology experts)

As a reminder we previously defined the following IS strategic areas of focus:

- Document Management
- Call Center Management

There needs to be one IS strategic team for each strategic area of focus. In this case there would be two teams. The strength of the IS strategic team is that it focuses energy and effort on one core strategy. By controlling the strategy and vision the team can confine activity and projects to those that are defined by and work with the strategy and vision. There will be no duplication of effort and no stray initiatives. The IS strategic team will also develop project and capital budget estimates and perform return on investment calculations, where appropriate. The team will then be able to manage and administer the resulting projects.

One benefit of both the IS strategic area of focus and the IS strategic team is that they are a convenient way to organize and address a large number of projects. This methodology provides a single vision with a defined path to arrive there. The best way to execute the defined strategy is through the IS strategic teams.

The IS strategic team will need to meet on a regularly scheduled basis. Initial meetings must be conducted to define the vision, the plan, and the schedules. The IS strategic team owner will then hold subsequent meetings to track progress and provide informational updates as needed.

B. Identify the Projects

Using the vehicle of the IS strategic teams, this is the creative step of turning all work to date into actionable projects. It requires a series of brainstorming and workshop sessions with the IS strategic team. It should take a number of days. Inputs created by this strategic exercise up to this point include the following:

- The business model
- The technology models
- The technology vision
- The strategic areas of focus
- The strategic drivers

The business members of the team will contribute the current and future anticipated business requirements. The IS team members will contribute all technology knowledge and previous technology research, as well as a structured way to deal with the requirements. This includes application package and industry technology knowledge, as well as a range of approaches and solutions that should be analyzed. The IS team members should also be responsible for bringing in various independent external integrators to make technology presentations and conduct informal educational seminars. Please exercise care here that the business does not jump to the stage of buying. The business should still be at the analysis stage. The business should not be vendor-sold or vendor-controlled. The outcome of this exercise will be a solidified vision within each strategic area of focus and a series of projects to realize that vision.

Let's use the document management strategic area of focus as an example. As a reminder, the definition of the area of focus was all systems (hardware and software) required to automate the document handling requirements needed to carry out the business. The vision developed was to implement an enterprise-wide, centralized document handling system with access from any desktop connected to the corporate network. The strategic area of focus included the following:

- **Activities** - document printing, document faxing, document imaging, document storage, document retrieval, document bar coding, and document handling
- **Documents** - claims, invoices, and any other printed, faxed, or electronic documents

We further defined that vision to include a detailed description of the new and relevant technologies. These included:

- **Document Imaging, Storage, and Retrieval** - Document imaging involves scanning the paper documents and storing the image electronically. These documents are indexed in such a way that agents can retrieve and display these images across the network on desktop devices.
- **Document Bar Coding** - Document bar coding involves printing specific data fields translated into bar codes. Documents are then exchanged between customers, physicians, and insurers. When returned, these documents are scanned and the bar code is electronically read.

The description of the technologies enabled us to identify and recommend conducting the following projects:

1. **Standardize Documents**
    Develop a standard way to store and retrieve documents, regardless of delivery vehicle.
2. **Document Printing**
    Centralize and standardize document printing. Reduce corporate printing costs by 10 percent.
3. **Document Imaging, Storage, and Retrieval**
    Centralize and image appropriate documents. Provide electronic storage and retrieval of document images. Eliminate the document filing room. Eliminate manual document searching and retrieval.

4. **Document Bar Coding**
   Deploy bar code printing and scanning of appropriate data fields with the goal of reducing or eliminating excessive document handling and keying of data. Reduce the cost of document handling and keying of data fields by 10 percent.
5. **Document Faxing**
   Centralize electronic, individual, and mass faxing or eliminate paper faxing where possible. Reduce paper faxing by 100 percent.
6. **Document Emailing**
   Centralize and standardize emailed documents.
7. **Electronic Interfaces**
   Centralize and standardize handling of electronic files and interfaces.

Using this example, the above sequence of work demonstrates how the strategic areas of focus can be translated into actionable projects. All projects can be identified and named.

C. Sequence the Projects

Next the projects need to be sequenced. This can be done in any number of ways by one of the following exercises:
- Start at the beginning process of the business model and work toward the end process in a linear fashion.
- Understand the dependencies between the projects and schedule the projects based on the interdependencies and sequencing requirements. This means installing foundation tools and technologies first and building on these.
- When dependencies and sequencing are not an impediment let the budget dictate the sequence. Do the projects when the business can afford them.
- Make sure the projects with the largest payback are done first or at least early in the strategy. This generates momentum and reinforces the value of the strategy.

Once the projects are sequenced the business can turn to project execution.

D. Execute the Projects

1. Execution

Managed by the IS strategic teams and using an appropriate project management methodology, IS will begin to execute these projects. Project execution presents two additional challenges. The first is project management and the second is project reporting. For project management I like to use a simple "plan, build, and run" methodology that I define in more detail in the subsequent business process approach. Please refer to that discussion in later chapters. Using the simple "plan, build, and run" methodology, develop project milestones for all projects. The milestone plan may look something like this:

- Plan:
    - ○ Create project charter scope document
    - ○ Create project schedule
- Build:
    - ○ Complete system design document
    - ○ Complete system acquisition
    - ○ Complete system testing
    - ○ Complete user acceptance testing
    - ○ Complete user training
    - ○ Complete limited pilot
    - ○ Complete documentation
    - ○ Complete installation and implement into production
- Run:
    - ○ Complete post-project review

It is important to match the level of project management formalization to the maturity of the organization. No matter how good the methodology, an unused methodology provides no value. I recommend keeping the methodology as simple as possible. Execute all of the essential project steps and produce standard repeatable deliverables. For simplicity I recommend Excel spreadsheets over MS project. To develop the proper milestones, map the project into the project management methodology.

Project management is but one challenge. Project and time reporting is another.

2. Project and Time Reporting

The IS strategic team has translated the strategy into projects and sequenced these projects into a project list. IS must now execute. It is critical that IS develops a project planning and reporting methodology that not only summarizes activity but accomplishes several tactical goals:

- Provides a weekly reference and status report for IS and the business
- Allows for both the studious and casual observer to easily check on project status
- Allows for project tracking by identified milestones
- Provides an inherent agenda for a regular review meeting
- Guides IS and the business to an exception-only focus
- Refocuses the business on what they should be doing and are doing on a regular basis
- Allows the business to change the direction and priority
- Forces shared ownership of the projects between IS and the business where it belongs
- Minimizes the time that must be spent on administrative project reporting

3. Time Tracking

Project planning and project reporting begins with time tracking. There is no way to manage what you can't measure. My experience is that time tracking measurements generally suffer from trying to measure too much or trying to measure the wrong things.

Speaking as an IS manager…here is what I need to know and this is all that I need to know. How much time is spent on the following?

- **Operations Support** - daily support in the form of maintenance and enhancements, including break/fix activities
- **New Project Work** - new development efforts tracking software development and infrastructure work separately
- **Administrative Time** - all lost and nonproductive time (including vacation, holidays, sick leave, and time lost to meetings and other administrative activities)

At a high level, knowing the hours in each of these three categories allows IS management to plan projects, track activities, and provide costs back to the business. IS management can show how time is spent and justify those expenditures. They can develop meaningful project estimates and provide a more accurate schedule of activities to the business. If IS management has a time tracking system that can provide these three simple measurements, they are poised to make use of the tools provided below. If not, IS management needs to buy and implement something promptly or modify their current time reporting to make these measurements immediately available. Time tracking is a critical component of project execution.

4. Project Estimates

Using the list of identified projects and the desired sequence of project execution, IS management must now establish their project estimates. IS management must develop project size estimates in man-hours at the project task level and in the aggregate. The point is to establish up-front what can be realistically expected of IS and determine what IS should realistically accomplish. The goal here is to identify the available IS development resources, decide where they will be deployed, and select what projects they can undertake. This is done by establishing a schedule of projects for a given time period. At a minimum, IS management needs to develop rough project estimates for each identified project in terms of broad man-hour estimates. This will foster some high-level planning and scheduling.

For a schedule, I recommend quarterly scheduling. Monthly is too short and anything longer than a quarter quickly becomes irrelevant. I recommend that IS conducts this exercise at the beginning of each quarter. Establish the quarterly schedule to coincide with the fiscal calendar and number the quarters as simply Q1 through Q4. These three components comprise the project estimating exercise:

- IS development capacity
- Project estimates
- Map estimates to capacity

5. Available Development Hours – Capacity

At the beginning of each quarter, IS management should begin by identifying their available development hours. This is, simply put, capacity. If IS management has a time reporting methodology in place, they can begin with how much time was devoted to new project development in the previous quarter. Let's use an example of 2,880 hours meaning IS reported 2,880 man-hours of time to new development projects last quarter. Next factor in any adjustments that must be made for the upcoming quarter based on known impacts such as staffing deletions, vacations, known support problems, or anything else affecting capacity for the coming quarter. These adjustments reduce or enhance the available capacity. Let's assume we lose 180 man-hours to vacations in the coming quarter. Then, for the sake of argument, let's say we add a development resource and can expect an additional 360 hours from that person. That would increase our capacity by 360 man-hours. Based on the staffing levels and extrapolation, we are able to calculate the estimated time to be spent on new development projects in the coming quarter. In our example that would be 3,060 man-hours. This is the IS development capacity from a planning perspective.

This exercise underscores the importance of tracking the time spent each quarter on the three broad service categories. For the initial quarter or when other data is not available, IS leadership may be forced to use an estimated number. I would use no more than 65 percent of the total available manpower hours for software development and no more than 25 percent for technology installation projects.

6. Project Delivery Schedules

Using the available capacity in man-hours, the proper sequencing of the projects, and the project estimates that have been developed, IS management may now establish the project delivery schedules. IS management may simply schedule the projects selected by the IS strategic team in sequence until the capacity is exhausted. Once this is accomplished, IS needs to share the schedule with the IS strategic team to get their buy in and support. I recommend an initial meeting at the beginning of each quarter. The outcome of that meeting should be a list of projects that can realistically be completed in the upcoming quarter. This project delivery schedule is the schedule that IS will now track to and report against.

E. Communications with the Business

1. IT Council Meetings

In order to communicate effectively with the business on project activity, IS leadership needs to establish a forum. I recommend establishment of an IT council with regularly scheduled weekly review meetings. The IT council will serve as the project governing and reporting body as well as the broker for the IS strategic teams and will resolve any priority or sequencing conflicts. The IT council will be comprised of the top business executives who are the primary stakeholders in the company. It needs to include the company officers (president, CFO, VP of marketing, and so on) and one to two levels of product or line management (GMs, directors, managers, and so on). It is important that the key decision makers and policy drivers are involved. The IT council should include all project sponsors as well as any business project managers. Most small organizations do not have dedicated project managers who just manage projects so most businesses get their project management personnel from among the business management. Project management should have the highest interest in the project activity.

I recommend a weekly meeting. Establish a regular time for the meetings. Take great pains to schedule the meeting at a time where IS can expect the most participation. Feed them if you must. The more participation, the better chance IS has of working on what is most important to the business. I have seen these meetings become poorly attended and eventually become irrelevant. This is a major danger signal. It implies that the projects have become unimportant to the business and business and technology focus is being centered outside of the endorsed projects and outside of IS.

2. Project Reporting

a. Detailed Reporting

Once the initial kickoff meeting is completed and the project schedule is defined, the real work begins. IS needs to develop and publish the detailed project delivery schedule based on previously defined project milestones. Here is the information IS needs to develop on each project:
- **Project number** - some reference number using a consecutively generated number, a month and year established, or any other common method for assigning numbers or values used in your business
- **Strategy** - identify which strategy the project is addressing
- **IS owner** - IS project owner
- **Sponsor** - business project sponsor
- **Milestones** - with due dates and statuses

To create a milestone plan take the major milestones and the project identification information from above and create a spreadsheet. This should be done using something simple like an Excel spreadsheet but nothing as complicated as MS Project. This becomes the detailed project reporting information for each project. For anyone interested in the project it should provide a detailed snapshot of how the project is being conducted.

Issue the spreadsheet weekly as the IS status report. On the project status line, use one of the following statuses:
- Pending
- Active
- Complete
- Cancelled
- Reforecast
- Color code the project status to reflect the following:
    - Green – project and milestones on schedule
    - Yellow – milestone in jeopardy, but project still on schedule
    - Red – milestone in jeopardy and project in jeopardy

- For the entry on the milestone line, use these statuses:
  - ᵒ Active
  - ᵒ Complete
  - ᵒ Reforecast
  - ᵒ Color code these statuses as well.

The focus of the IT council meeting should be on the yellow and red statuses. All participants should attempt to prevent discussion on the green status projects. For green status projects, reference the project documents and encourage the requestor to take the discussion off-line with the IS leadership. The meeting must not become a general discussion or complaint session but a progress reporting session. Discuss the reasons that the project went yellow or red. Discuss the steps IS leadership is taking to get the project back on schedule. IS should reforecast the dates if they must but should not make this a regular exercise or IS loses credibility. Reforecast dates for a project no more than once during a quarter. Do not reforecast dates for more than one project at a meeting or IS credibility again comes into question. The goal here is to communicate early and often and not let projects meander down to a deadline before they become discussion topics and get corrective attention.

b. Summary Reporting

As a cover sheet for the detailed report, IS leadership needs to develop a one-page summary of the project progress. This summary will convey the progress throughout the quarter at a glance. It should be viewed as a status report document that can be shared with anyone in the business to depict project status. I recommend that IS report projects that are in the following statuses on this page:
- Projects removed (completed or cancelled)
- Projects on the watch list (yellow and red status projects)
- Candidate projects (projects identified as important after the quarter starts but not yet formalized enough to make the project list)
- Projects activated (projects identified and added to the list during the quarter)

This should be set up as a one-page spreadsheet that is also color coded. I would include for each project on the list:
- Project name
- Project number
- Date added or removed
- Sponsor
- Reason or explanation

3. Brokering Priorities – Adding and Removing Projects

IS leadership needs to provide a structured process for adding and removing projects from the project list. Since all projects must fit within the published strategy, adding and removing projects must be done with great care and must be part of the overall strategic focus. This needs to be a visible and accessible process. IS leadership will need to publish this process, constantly refer back to it, and reference it throughout the course of their discussions with the IS strategic team and the IT council. Here is where changes to the strategy can be made if they are understood and agreed upon by all. Please reference appendix 7.1 for a sample process flow.

III. Summary

These tactics work. They have been battle tested and used successfully. Each step is critical to understanding and managing the execution of the business model strategy.

Business Model and the Individual

Chapter 8

WISDOM to work by

1. *Retooling may be necessary.*

2. *Technology specialists and project managers are critical.*

3. *Structure and methodology become more important.*

4. *Consider organizing first around two groups:*
   a. *Infrastructure*
   b. *Applications*

5. *Implement an environment and foster a mentality emphasizing service.*

6. *You cannot manage what you do not measure. Implement scorecards and key performance indicators.*

I. INTRODUCTION

As with retooling the technology from a strategic and tactical perspective, the business must also retool the existing IS management and staff. The approach and the personnel the business used to get them here will fail to carry them through this next barrier.

II. THE INDIVIDUAL

The business will need stronger technology people. By that I mean it needs experienced experts in each area of the strategic focus areas. Using the examples given, the business needs document management experience in that area and call center experience in that area. The business needs someone familiar with the target technologies to cut down on the learning curve and to save on research and development time. The business needs people who understand what can and cannot be done with the various technologies. The business will also have heavy vendor reliance once external independent integrator studies are done and technology solutions are selected.

IS will need employees who are also highly skilled in structured analysis. IS will need employees who can manage formal analysis and selection of both infrastructure components and application package solutions. Buying without proper due diligence based on vendor relationships or other shortsighted reasons is always disastrous. IS needs employees who can take each of the projects and do the following:

- Research the available technologies to understand what is feasible.
- Select the appropriate sized solution set; e.g., small, medium or large.
- Identify the possible solutions.
- Limit and scope the solutions.
- Research the functions and features of the possible solutions.
- Evaluate the solutions by meaningful comparisons and some quantitative analysis.
- Visit customer sites where technology is installed and understand the solutions at work.
- Select, negotiate, and purchase the solution.
- Install and monitor the solution.

The business also needs, within IS, the acceptance of the next higher vision. This is one of service. This vision begins with the definition of a service philosophy and the service pyramid. It continues with service delivery and service delivery vehicles. It culminates with service tracking and the resulting measurements that must ultimately lead to service improvement.

All of the things discussed during the previous business layer strategy apply at this level as well. For management and staff, many will not make the transition from the layered approach (which requires the identified generalist skill sets) to the model approach (which requires a more specific technology skill set). Please reread those sections and select the approach given below to restructure the department.

III. THE ORGANIZATION

I find it convenient at this organization size to have two simple groups. One is an infrastructure group that deals with all technologies and technology support while the other is an applications group that deals with software, packages, development, and applications support. The infrastructure group consists primarily of the following skill groups:

- Infrastructure/telephony/server engineers
- Production database administrators (DBAs)
- Computer operators
- Service/help desk technicians
- Desktop technicians

The application group consists primarily of the following skill groups:

- Programmers/programmer analysts/system analysts
- Development DBAs
- Package experts
- Business analysts
- Software testers

- Project managers

One group leader for each will suffice for a management structure.

A. Service Statement

The business must enable the entire IS department to understand and adopt a service mentality. While it is mainly about the technology in this strategy, it is also about the service. I have developed a service pyramid conveying the philosophy in a pictorial format that fosters understanding and acceptance. It is included as appendix 8.1.

1. Service Level 1

The pyramid base is comprised of daily operations support and servicing existing customers. For a typical company, it might include the following:
- Systems and services availability
- Break/fix activities
- Troubleshooting and problem solving
- Nightly batch processing completion
- Services and support for existing customers

The goal here is to protect and support what the business has already constructed. At a minimum, this should keep the business operating smoothly.

2. Service Level 2

The next level up allows for improvements on the current situation by tactically performing well on projects, clients, and tasks. For a typical company, that might include the following:
- Enhancements or improvements of existing client support or services
- Improved communication and performance between IS and the business
- Project performance through good project management and delivery
- Simple functionality improvements
- Small measurable improvements in timing or pricing

The goal here is to improve within the existing business constraints and business systems by providing better price/performance ratios or economies of scale.

3. Service Level 3

At the top of the pyramid, we include strategic improvements that drastically change the scope and nature of the business. These include acquiring new customers and executing new projects that substantially change the product or service offerings of the business. It might include, at a minimum, any of the following:
- Buying and installing new infrastructure
- Buying or building new software application systems

- Implementing a new strategic initiative
- Entering a new market
- Addressing a new set of customers
- Changing the process flow of a major component of the business

The goal here is to strategically improve on the business in terms of revenue and profitability.

B. Service Delivery

1. Service Philosophy

To enact the service philosophy, IS leadership and staff must understand what they do and the importance of those things to the business. I find it convenient to classify and track the types of work that IS does into the following categories:
- Daily production support
- Process and performance improvements
- Long-term infrastructure and new development projects

This is slightly different than the time tracking approach.
- **Operations support** - maintenance and enhancements including break/ fix activities
- **New project work** - development and infrastructure tracked separately
- **Administrative time** - all lost and nonproductive time including vacation, holidays, sick leave, and time lost to meetings and other administrative activities

It is necessary to reconcile the two when looking at operations support work.

For a company this size at this time I recommend a basic work ticketing system that should be used for all work. There are several inexpensive options available. Buy a basic inexpensive solution. The key is to get all work in one place and to track all work religiously. Classify each ticket in relationship to the pyramid and classify each for time tracking purposes. IS now has one place to do all of their tracking and reporting.

2. Daily Service Reminders

IS leadership must control the way work enters and leaves the department. They must block the activities that always occur that are not documented and not prioritized. IS leadership should set it up so that all work goes to a central service desk or a desig-nated service desk person. They should enter all work into a ticketing system and assign and prioritize work daily. IS leadership can then report on that work constructively. IS leadership must find a way to minimize disruptions to the staff and control what gets done. They can use the service pyramid in the prioritization process. IS will struggle to work effectively with the business until both groups understand the service process and the service priorities.

One early challenge is service availability. If IS starts each day by responding to inquiries about production status or production availability, they are wasting a lot of productive time. IS leadership should be proactive and develop something that answers these questions such as the simplified report defined as appendix 8.2. This is a daily systems availability communication plan that communicates status on outages and availability. IS can train the business to look here for their answers thereby avoiding numerous calls and interruptions.

C. Service Tracking

1. IS Scorecards

One quick and easy way to track service performance is to set up a monthly or quarterly IS scorecard. Please reference appendix 8.3 for a sample scorecard format that I find useful. The purpose of the scorecard is to measure performance to plans in a quantitative way. I recommend that IS leadership use the service pyramid to set up the categories and values. Be realistic. If priorities change, which they are apt to do, IS leadership should be allowed to make some minor adjustments to the scoring. It is important to review these with the staff both before and after each performance period. I also like to post them in a conspicuous place so that business partners and visitors have access.

2. IS Key Performance Indicators (KPIs)

Another method for service performance tracking is to set up key performance indicators, or KPIs, and match performance against them. This can be either a narrative exercise or IS leadership can build a spreadsheet to track performance. Again, please reference the service pyramid to develop the indicators and to develop simple but meaningful metrics. Some good examples include the following measurements:
- Systems availability – 99 percent
- Nightly batch processing completion by 8:00 a.m. daily – 100 percent
- Project milestones met – 80 percent

The key here is to begin to measure the performance in some reasonable and quantitative way. Start with the basics – the things that are easy to quantify and capture – and build on it over time. IS leadership should go to the IS strategic teams or the IT council to identify problems or issues they feel are important to track. Make the indicators relevant to the bottom line of the business. For example, technology being unavailable has a direct impact on revenue. Find out what other direct relationships exist between technology and the business. Use these to provide relevant performance measurements.

IV. SUMMARY

To succeed with this strategy the business will need different skill sets and probably different individuals. IS leadership will need the proper organization structure fitting the service delivery methods that are being recommended. IS will need to focus heavily on both technology and service. IS leadership must begin to develop measurements and metrics to support how they are performing. IS leadership can also educate the IS staff on the direct business impacts of IS performance.

Growth Level 3

> **WISDOM to work by:**
>
> 1. *One size does not fit all. No single strategy and no strategy enactment works forever.*
> 2. *The business and the IS department will surely reach another barrier.*
> 3. *The business model strategy has a technology-centric focus and necessarily ignores process.*
> 4. *Again, the things the business had done to get them here are the things that begin to work against them.*
> 5. *Process, process, process—boring, but critical!*

I. INTRODUCTION

The business model approach will take the business only so far. This strategic approach with its primary focus on technology will lead to another failure event. This failure event may vary by industry, market, or company but the event will inevitably occur. The business model approach was necessarily technology focused. Due to growth in the business and an increase in the number of employees, technology—while still the critical component—eventually becomes less of an impediment than the internal business and IS processes. I know this is unusual to hear coming from the IS organization but technology is not always the answer. The resulting state will be an environment characterized by a total lack of process focus. This will present stunning and debilitating internal issues for both the business and IS. The business model strategy necessarily ignores process and process improvements. The business previously needed technology in all areas of the business and the business model strategy delivered. What the strategy did not contain was an enterprise-wide integration approach or one where all technology components are made to work cohesively together.

Congratulations to the business. It has reached the third hurdle. It will be character-ized by the following states: due to conflicting roles and responsibilities, IS service and support is inconsistent and unacceptable. Relationships between the business and IS are strained despite major improvements in technology. The IS group appears to be too large, too expensive, and too unwieldy. IS views itself as a technology organization and not a service organization. The business is running well on the legacy technology systems but informality in process and procedures is rampant. The business investment in IS continues to grow and the return on investment continues to diminish. The business may again be experiencing turnover in IS management and staff. It appears that the business must use consulting resources in order to get things done. The business is again at a critical juncture in organizational growth.

In short, the business was successful using the business model approach but IS is once again struggling. The growth has been exciting but likely unbridled. The business added staff and technical solutions to a technology based organization with little thought to the resulting organization structure or to the identification and clarity of internal processes. Simply put, a process based approach is missing from both the business and the IS department. There are conflicting roles and responsibilities and substantial departmental overlap. The business has no built-in efficiencies and few economies of scale. Somewhere at this next barrier, the business is quite naturally stymied again.

II. STRATEGY

From a strategic perspective, the business model approach as a strategy will have been effective. This approach has some built-in shortcomings because the business vision that supported it was focused solely on technology in general and the specific technologies that were required to build the business. Now that the business has the proper technologies and the proper solution sets in place, it needs to look internally at the people and processes performing the work. The focus needs to be on organizational realignment and process engineering. The business needs to find ways to clarify functions and departments. The business must find ways to distinctly define all of the roles and responsibilities. This is accomplished by analyzing the business from a process perspective and by adopting a process reengineering approach. The business must do away with the specific people dependencies and get the business knowledge and business rules out of everyone's heads and into documentation. The shortcomings are fueled by the failure of the business and IS to recognize that a process approach, instead of a technology approach, is now needed. The business model approach does not allow for the requisite revamping and fine-tuning of the way the business operates.

III. TACTICS

The business symptoms that will be experienced are as follows:
The business has added many employees and most likely many more products and services. IS has greatly increased the number of technology solutions and business appli-cations. The business has increased in both size and complexity. The customer base has

increased as well and the business has locked up and finalized for now the core products or services. The business is likely moving into a more mature slow-growth phase. The business has even more money to spend but there is even greater internal competition for the dollars. The business has a steady and growing piece of the market and growth is most likely in larger chunks as the business competes for and wins more business. The business has more time to react to clients but doesn't necessarily respond any better. It now has numerous large clients. There is an opportunity to set the bar in their market. The business is realizing some economies of scale but not nearly enough. Operationally, the business continues to do things sloppily and to make mistakes with clients; none of which are large, but in the aggregate cause the business great concern. The business is growing but has reached another difficult barrier. The business is considering some huge investments in internal systems and solutions like customer relationship management basically looking for a technology panacea instead of a process or organizational solution.

The business has reached hurdle three. It is characterized primarily by the business knowing that there are specific process and procedural impediments but not knowing what to deploy or what to embrace. IS has the core technologies in place but the company is rife with duplicate functions and inefficiencies. The business leadership has the uneasy feeling that IS is doing the wrong projects and the wrong things. The IS group has grown substantially but still lacks form and function. IS is not responsive on smaller issues and most exchanges with them are not satisfactory or successful. IS is starting to experience employee turnover in both management and staff.

IV. THE INDIVIDUAL

The IS symptoms that will be experienced are as follows:

IS is not organized properly to service the business. There is much overlap and confusion surrounding roles and responsibilities. Only the "fun" stuff seems to get done. IS is being pushed to consider larger and broader solutions but daily service and support is nagging and consuming most of their time. IS suspects that the requests for functionality enhancements are adding little to no value to the business. IS has a reputation for lousy service due to the structure of the department and the technology focus that has been required. The staff has reached a size that is unmanageable under the current organization structure and management team. IS is no longer nimble or responsive since their internal processes and procedures seem to work against them rather than for them. IS still spends a large amount of time supporting legacy systems and propping up existing technologies. IS can't seem to effect change without service interruptions or negative impacts to the business. If the business had to characterize the department, they would say IS has the wrong skill sets doing the wrong things in the wrong ways. IS is still people-centric and people-dependent with vacations and illnesses wreaking havoc with service delivery. IS is in no way process-dependent or process-centric. Leadership changes are common and staff turnover is frequent.

V. SUMMARY

Once again, the IS department has become an impediment to the business and not an asset. But in this case they are suffering from the same symptoms as the business itself. Those symptoms are process inefficiency and poor service due to organization mishaps and conflicting roles and responsibilities. Once again, in the defined business cycle, this is not an unusual occurrence. This is a normal and natural outcome of the business growth cycle. This barrier will be hit. The business model approach is sound and effective but the technology focus brings the business naturally to process inefficiencies. The technology approach has outlived its usefulness. The previous strategy did provide an excellent foundation on which to build. Due to the success of implementing the right technologies, the business is facing process—not technology—challenges. The business now needs an entirely different focus and needs to go about the strategic approach in a different way. It is time for the business to take the foot off the technology accelerator pedal and put it to the process brake pedal. It is time for the business process approach.

Business Process Strategy

I. INTRODUCTION

The business process approach is a structured and comprehensive approach that involves an in-depth analysis of the processes, department organization and technology architecture within the IS organization. Please reference appendix 10.1 (Business Process Approach – Strategy) that summarizes this approach. These three components—a strategic trilogy, if you will—provide the framework with which to tackle the barriers that have been encountered. It first focuses on defining the processes within IS. It turns to a reorganization of the IS department to align with and support those processes. It culminates with a reexamination and definition of the technology architecture which provides the overriding guidelines for treating technology going forward. While technology is still a critical component it now becomes one of three different focus areas. While IS is first and foremost a technology organization, this singular focus is itself creating the barrier. Only by creating a process focus and a process vision, and aligning the IS organization with that vision, will the business be able to move to the next level. The goal must be to address technology as a process-centric organization. All of the outputs from the tools and techniques used in the business model approach are useful here and provide good reference material.

The business process strategy approach is much more formal and structured than previous approaches. It has been devised from exposure and experience with larger businesses and larger IS organizations. No matter what the size of the IS organization all businesses face the same challenges. The strategic process follows a by now predictable pattern.

- Assessment
- Strategy
- Execution and monitoring

The assessment exercise includes using numerous tools and techniques to define where the IS department is currently positioned. Next the exercise determines where the IS department needs to go. Then it is time to execute. The essence of this strategy has the following framework. I refer to these as the strategic trilogy.

- IS processes and process reengineering
- IS organization and organization realignment
- Technology architecture

II. STRATEGY

A. Assessment

1. Introduction

This entire strategic exercise assumes the business has clearly defined the business direction and has communicated this direction clearly to the IS department. It is an IS-centric series of exercises with direct impact and benefit to the business. The business leadership needs to be actively driving this strategy for it to be successful. If existing IS leadership is capable of expanding into a much larger role, they should take ownership. If not, please refer to the later chapter of this strategy on the individual and come back to this assessment after new leadership has been selected.

To begin, the IS department has to know where it is today. It would be convenient to have one of those little terrain maps found in shopping malls with an arrow that points to a spot marked "You Are Here." Unfortunately the IS team has to build that map themselves. The IS department must go through a series of strategic assessment exercises to determine and document the status of the department. This is the jumping -off point for the entire strategic exercise. It involves applying various tried and true tools and techniques to measure the quality of the existing information services delivery and performance. Included below are some common tools and techniques I have used. I take no credit for their creation. Where possible, for clarity, I have provided sample results. The business and IS management should select from this set of tools and use any or all of them until they are satisfied that they have a true picture of the challenge being faced. The goal is to honestly and accurately take stock of the IS department and document the results.

2. Positional Analysis

This is a series of narratives describing the position of the business and the position of IS within the business. Use the samples given to construct a narrative that describes the specific positions of IS and the business.

a. External Position

Prepare a narrative describing the position of both the business and the IS department in external terms. Include statements about market position, financial situation and products and services for the business. Compare the IS position against competitors in the marketplace. Example statements might include something like the following:
- We hold current competitive positions in two distinct markets.
- We have established ourselves as a market leader but are seen as a "me too" company in the technology arena.
- We are financially viable but have limited budget for IS spending.

b. Business Position

Prepare a narrative describing the business position in terms of business focus, lines of business, capabilities, core competencies and strategic direction. Example statements might include the following:
- The business focus has been on customers classified as SMBs. We have not approached the Fortune 500 market.
- Our core competencies are found in inbound call centers, not outbound.
- We have little expertise in the printing market but our customers are suggesting we give it a try.

c. IS Position

Prepare a narrative describing the view of IS within the organization from the perspective of the business. Focus on issues like effectiveness, capabilities and communication. Also prepare a narrative describing the technology state of the department regarding applications, platforms, networks, data, security, staffing, personnel, capacities and facilities. Example statements might include some thing like the following:
- We are seen as order takers and not legitimate business partners.
- We gain consensus only to see the business ignore us two weeks later and move in another direction.
- Our platforms are stable and always available.
- Our department has a poor record of project management.
- We have underlying issues of data security.

3. Situational Analysis

The following set of tools is meant to be used to formally document the current situation within IS. None are new or particularly creative. They attempt to get participants to do an honest assessment. Most should be done in a narrative form. I have provided samples for clarity where possible.

a. SWOT Analysis

List IS strengths, weaknesses, opportunities and threats. Examples might include the following:
- Strengths
  - Good business knowledge
  - Strong technical competence
- Weaknesses
  - Documentation is poor
  - Project management methodology is too informal
- Opportunities
  - Platforms are stable and we can build upon them
  - Poor economy makes IS talent available and affordable
- Threats
  - The business believes outsourcing is the solution
  - We do not have enough support from frontline managers

b. Critical Success Factors

List the things that the IS department must do particularly well to align with the business and be successful. Examples might include the following:
- We have to communicate much better within the internal IS department.
- We must become strong at project management.
- We should establish workable and productive relationships with the sales team.
- We need to get control of the desktop.

c. Root Cause Analysis

Take the five or six most common complaints about IS. Analyze them from both a business and an IS perspective. Delve into the root causes. The observer should see some trends. Examples might include the following:
- **Complaint:** IS does not provide good daily service and support.
- **Analysis:** This complaint harks back to us relying on engineers to provide service and support after installation. The engineers have already moved on to the next project and have no time to provide that support.
- **Root Cause 1:** We are not providing adequate documentation or training.
- **Root Cause 2**: We are not organized properly or staffed properly to provide this level of support.

d. Core Competency Analysis

List the top five or six core competencies that are required and map the IS existing capabilities to these competencies. It would be excellent if these could be matched to the business model prepared in the previous sections. Examples might include the following:
- **Billing** - We are excellent at billing. Our systems are sound and we have a good understanding of the business billing requirements within our department.
- **Document Management** - We are very strong at document management. Our systems are world-class and we continue to expand on the applications.

e. Alignment Analysis

Construct a matrix with the individual IS departmental groups on one axis and the departments they serve on the other. Describe how these groups interact, communicate and deliver services. Focus on failures or misalignments. Please see appendix 10.2 for a sample of a misaligned IS department.

f. Technology Forecasting

List the top five or six technologies that have the most critical impact on the business. These should mirror the technologies identified in the business model strategic approach. Define the impact, the extent to which these technologies have been leveraged, the future direction of the technologies and what IS can do to prepare for those changes. Try using a narrative scenario approach or redo the strategic exercises given in the technology model approach. Examples might include the following:
- **Call Center Technologies**
  We continue to provide inbound call center services to our customers. More and more we are being asked to bundle these services with outbound call center services. We have not exploited these opportunities. We predict that outbound call center technologies are the key to our future. The differences between inbound and outbound can be found in the predictive dialer technologies. These are software and hardware systems that work in conjunction with the primary phone system. They eliminate wait times for agents between calls and allow us to speak to five times more clients on behalf of our customers.

g. Value Chain Analysis

Analyze the translation of resources into functionality within IS. Analyze the way functionality is requested and how services and resources are deployed to satisfy functionality requests. An abbreviated example might include something like the following:

- **Project management**
  - ⁰ Current value chain:
    - The business decides to do a project.
    - The business kicks off the project.
    - The business works on the project until if flounders.
    - The business calls IS to get the project back on track.
  - ⁰ Proposed value chain:
    - We establish, publish and follow a simple methodology.
    - We recognize a need.
    - We establish a sponsor, a team and an IS lead.
    - We gather requirements.
    - We design a solution.
    - We start a project.
    - We report progress regularly in a standard format.
    - We complete the project.
    - We install the results.
    - We conduct a post-mortem to improve the process.

h. Benchmarking

Compare the performance of the IS department to market leaders in various other markets and against the closest competition in the market. This might take some research and discussions with various business leaders but examples might include something like the following:

- **Against our competition:** We are never first to market with new products. This is due to our poor project management methodology and the inability to respond to customer needs in a timely manner. We need to establish a steering committee where we discuss what our competitors are doing in the marketplace and find a way to get in front of our customers' needs. We need to be proactive instead of reactive. We need to shorten our project delivery cycle for new functionality by improving upon our methodology and processes. This is a business challenge as well as an IS challenge.

B. The Strategy Itself

1. Introduction

The business and IS management can now use what has been learned during the assessment phase to chart the new course. This series of steps builds on the conclusions that are drawn from the assessment exercises. The goal is to determine where IS needs to go and what they need to do to get there. It involves determining where the IS department needs to be in order to support the business imperatives. This is a galvanizing exercise!

In some cases IS management needs to simply refer to what they have learned during the assessment phase. In others they have some additional work to do. The business and IS management must set up the target state for the department. First, IS management must provide the process and procedural definitions and ways to capitalize on process reengineering efforts. Then, IS management must determine how to organize and look at their organizational realignment options. Last, IS management must define the broad technology architecture vision, direction and guidelines.

2. Conclusions

Based on the observations and narrative from both the situational analysis and the positional analysis, the business and IS management can identify eight to ten conclusions about the effectiveness, or lack thereof, of the IS department. Use the format below to document and explain them.

- Observation Statement and Description
- Root Cause – the source of the problem
- Supporting Evidence
- Possible Actions/Strategic Moves

An abbreviated example might include something like this:

- Observation: The IS position within the business is very weak.
- Root Cause: Due to personalities and performance our IS leadership has not built the proper relationships and aligned themselves tightly with the business leadership.
- Supporting Evidence: Projects are initiated without IS collaboration. IS is not invited to business strategy meetings. IS is being treated as order takers.
- Strategic Moves: Rebuild the relationship by a series of proactive moves. These include building the business model and technology models and sharing these with the business. Also, begin monthly luncheon meetings hosted by IS management for business management where performance and direction are discussed openly and honestly. Develop ways for the leadership to interact more often and more significantly.

3. Critical Issues and Strategic Moves

a. Critical Issues

Armed with these conclusions, the business and IS management can now develop the critical issues and strategic moves to address them. At a minimum, IS management should consider addressing critical issues in some of the following areas:

- **Relationships** - Discuss IS relationships with the business specifically for sales, marketing, operations, production, human resources, accounting and finance. Discuss the internal IS relationships between groups, leaders and associates. Example statements might include something like the following:
  - Our IS infrastructure manager and the sales manager both golf but they have not established open communications. We need to get them out on the golf course together so they can establish a foundation for a productive business relationship.

- Our IS team is not speaking with one voice and supporting each other. They need a series of team-building relationships to get them to work as one team. Otherwise, we need to change out certain leadership positions.
- **Leadership** – Evaluate the IS leadership team. An example might read like this:
  - Our CIO has not built the required relationship with the other senior leadership. This needs to happen immediately if we are going to be successful.
- **Budgets** – Discuss IS budget restraints and budget composition. An example might read like this:
  - **Training Budget** - Our training budget is much too small. We need to convince the business leadership that training is a necessary investment and not an expense.
- **Platforms** – Develop a spreadsheet showing legacy situations and areas where improvements and expenditures must be made. An example might read like this:
  - **Telephone System** - Our telephone system is so old that we cannot find the add-on functionality that we need in the area of inbound call management. Due to some new client requirements we need more sophisticated automated call distribution functionality.
- **Technologies** - Discuss existing technology use and strategic directions that relevant technologies must take. Focus on open systems, desktops, interfaces, databases, the Internet and technologies specific to the industry. As example might match the following:
  - **Call Centers** – We need to do research and development on outbound call center technologies. We need to focus on the outbound predictive dialer technology which has numerous benefits to the business.
- **Architecture** – The organization is at a size such that a discussion of architecture is critical. Develop definitions, architecture principles and architecture guidelines. This narrative should include the following sections:
  - Introduction
  - Executive summary
  - Key issues and observations (technology focus areas)
  - Assessment of current situation (by technology)
  - Architecture design principles
  - Strategies
  - Standards and products
  - Technology architecture statements (by technology)
  - Summary
- **Capacities** - Show IS limiting factors and barriers to growth within infrastructure, networks and applications. An example might be like this:
  - We have limited bandwidth on the wide area network. We cannot push the existing document management applications reliably to the branches. This is causing lost information and disruptions to the business. We need to expand the bandwidth on the wide area network.
- **Planning** - Evaluate the IS planning processes and procedures with a goal of instilling a structured planning process and provide for appropriate staffing. This strategic planning effort requires staffing and a commitment. It might

include the following:
- ◦ Budgeting processes (capital and expense)
- ◦ Manpower estimates
- ◦ Purchasing standards and procedures
- ◦ Process reengineering
- **Growth** - Match the internal IS growth plans to the business plans. The business will provide the business plans.
- **Organization, manpower, and staffing** - This requires a full evaluation of the human resource side of the IS department and is the prelude to the organization and realignment exercise. Please refer to the sections on organization and realignment.
- **Facilities and services** - Detail any limiting factors here. Include location and floor space. This should include everything from office space to server rooms. Discuss locations of employees and what that does to communication and performance.
- **Applications** - Develop a spreadsheet showing how each legacy application serves specific business processes. Refer to the business model and technology model approach used in the business model strategy. Focus on inhibitors.
- **Projects** - Prepare a list of existing and future IS projects. Reexamine their applicability to the assessment and the strategy exercise that is being performed. Please refer to the projects discussion in the business model approach.

b. Strategic Moves

Using the issues, define the required actions or moves. Using the bullet points below, define the specific things that IS must now do to make the organization a success. Sequence these and develop a milestone plan with activities and deliverables. This is a natural outgrowth of the assessment. Some abbreviated examples might include the following:
- We must define and implement a project management methodology that suits our environment at this point in time.
  - ◦ Q1 – **research options; conduct a make or buy study**
  - ◦ Q2 – introduce to the business and gain buy in
  - ◦ Q3 – roll out the methodology
  - ◦ Q3 – assure that we use methodology on all projects
- We must establish the IS steering committee and get commitment from the business to make it work.
  - ◦ Jan. – meet with CEO and gain acceptance
  - ◦ Feb. – meet with other senior leadership and gain acceptance
  - ◦ Mar.– define roles, responsibilities, ground rules, schedules and expectations
  - ◦ Apr. – hold first meeting
- We must install a work ticketing application immediately.
  - ◦ Week 1 – research options (assume buy)
  - ◦ Week 2 – test options

- ○ Week 3 – choose package
- ○ Week 4 – buy and install package
- ○ Week 5 – begin to use package

4. The Strategic Trilogy – The Strategic Framework

The business and IS management can now organize the strategic issues and strategic moves by asking the questions given below. These broad focus areas provide the framework for organizing and executing the strategy.
- What processes do we perform?
- Who in IS performs these processes?
- How do we in IS perform them?

a. IS Processes and IS Process Reengineering

This first third of the trilogy involves the business processes within IS and between IS and the business. To remove the barriers and move to the next level, IS management must understand and focus on these processes. The ultimate goal will be to achieve improvements in performance, cost, quality, service and speed.

Each business or IS process is a collection of activities that takes one or more inputs and creates an output of value to IS or the business. Perform the following exercise:

Strategic Exercise:

- Identify and list the major IS processes.
- Describe the IS processes, sub-processes and related procedures.
- Create an organization structure to support the processes.
- Assign overall responsibility for the process or sub-process.
- Define detailed and specific roles and responsibilities.
- Create an environment that supports the roles and responsibilities.

Allow me to work through an example to show you what I mean. At a high level, it is convenient to define most of the major IS processes as shown in the following list. The IS department may need to add more to this list as they move through the exercise or IS can easily work with these.

Identify and List the Major IS Processes:

These are the major processes that IS should focus on in any IS organization:
- **Plan**
- **Build**
- **Run**

Identify and List the Major IS Sub-processes:

From the major processes, IS management can identify most of their specific sub-processes:
- **Planning**
- **Budgeting**
- **Architecture/Infrastructure engineering**
- **Infrastructure support (break/fix)**
- **Applications development**
- **Applications purchasing**
- **Applications installation**
- **Applications support (break/fix)**
- **Project management**
- **Computer operations**
- **Systems administration**
- **User communication**
- **Technology purchasing**
- **Asset management**

Identify and List the Major IS Sub-sub-processes:

IS management can then break down each of these into sub-sub-processes.
- **Planning:**
    Aligning IS with the business
    Technology planning
    Project portfolio planning
- **Budgeting:**
    Capital budgeting
    Expense budgeting
- **Architecture/Infrastructure engineering:**
    Architecture vision
    Architecture strategy
    Architecture definition
    Architecture research and development
    Architecture selection and identification
    Architecture installation
    Architecture configuration
    Third-tier support
- **Infrastructure support (break/fix):**
    First-tier support
    Second-tier support
- **Applications development:**
    Requirements gathering
    Application design
    Application coding
    Application testing

Application installation
Application modification
- **Applications purchasing:**
   Requirements gathering
   Identifying options
   Investigating options
   Developing selection criteria
   Performing evaluation
   Selecting solution
   Testing solution
   Installing solution
   Supporting solution
- **Applications support (break/fix):**
   First-tier support
   Second-tier support
- **Project management:**
   Plan activities
   Build activities
   Run activities
- **Computer operations:**
   Monitor nightly batch processing
   Manage printing
   Manage system backups
   Manage job priorities
   Manage computing environment
- **Systems administration:**
   Monitor system performance
   Manage system resources
   Manage capacity planning
- **User communication:**
   Handle outbound communications to users
   Handle inbound communications to users
- **Technology purchasing:**
   Manage technology expense budget
   Manage vendor relationships
   Manage technology acquisition
- **Asset management:**
   Manage inventory
   Tag inventory
   Asset disposal

Describe the IS Processes:

That completes the identifying and listing portion of the exercise. Now IS management can use the process and procedure templates given in appendix

10.3 to document the IS processes, sub-processes, sub-sub-processes and all of the related procedures. I will not go through each one of these but IS management can use the forms provided to develop the process definitions. This will give IS management an in-depth understanding of their process responsibilities and what these responsibilities entail. The logical next step is to assign responsibility for the process step and define roles and responsibilities. Before IS management can assign process responsibilities, they must address the organization structure. I will return to this process discussion after the following organization discussion.

b. IS Organization and Realignment

This is the second segment of the trilogy and should be addressed before IS management can complete the process exercise. The discussion of process should have allowed IS management to make some important observations about the existing organization structure and its lack of suitability for addressing and managing the major IS processes. The overriding message is the need to reorganize and realign around the identified IS processes.

Let me use the example of IS communication. One of the major problems with any IS department is controlling the projects and activities of the staff. This is usually compounded by the endless informal ways that the IS team comes into contact with the business. These channels for interaction are numerous. Each business team, from sales to accounting, has contacts they use within the IS organization. This communication and the resulting work requests must be handled. In many cases, it is unproductive. Even when it is productive, it often produces the wrong results. These communications result in unplanned activities and projects. Even more disconcerting, these activities never get recorded or tracked. This is the informal way that work gets done. It is basically undocumented and unmanageable. IS management should recognize that there needs to be a rigid, controlled process whereby the business user makes a formal work request of IS. IS management needs to define, document and hold someone responsible for this process.

The Technology and People Based Organization

At this point in time, I am certain that IS is a technology based organization focused around the various technologies. IS has a server group, a network group, a telecom group and so on. Each technology group owns all of the processes surrounding their technologies. That in itself is the problem. Please reference appendix 10.4 showing a typical technology based organization structure.

The technology based organization is built around technology skill sets. In it one group is responsible for each technology. This structure works until the maintenance and support load gets so large that day-to-day support will begin to drastically suffer. When given a choice, engineers will choose to do what they enjoy and not what the user needs. Engineers will work on new project after new project and stop picking up the phone once that new project is done. Questions, problems and support sink to the bottom of the To-Do list. Is it any wonder that the organization is seen as non-responsive? Who wants to do support? The result is that nine out of ten of the IS interactions (read opportunities) to support the business go unresolved. This is critically wrong! This situation leads us directly to the need to organize around process and have an IS group that is responsible for user interactions and user communications. That's why help desks were invented. The process of satisfying the user needs goes directly to the help desk.

The Process Based Organization

The process based organization is the answer to the question of how IS should organize to best support the identified IS processes. Referencing each of the processes previously listed above, we have the following:
- **Plan** - planning, project management, capital budgeting, purchasing, asset management, vendor relationships
- **Build** - software development and infrastructure construction
- **Run** - computer operations, IS production processes, user services, user communications, user support, second-level support, maintenance

Each of these broad process categories are then dissected into smaller categorizations and a single group is held responsible for each process. Please reference appendix 10.5 for a process based organization structure.

This structure will allow IS to define and document how they will deal with users, provide services, arbitrate priorities, communicate, manage projects, meet service level agreements, report on key performance indicators, implement IS scorecards, recruit talent, build a knowledge base and implement technologies. IS management can now develop IS process responsibilities using the new model.

The process based organization works. I have implemented it several times and it always solves a number of basic problems. It allows for process ownership, improves performance and provides distinct career paths. I will expound on this during the execution discussion.

Organization and Realignment

Now IS management can document the required new organization structure. Use the process model attachment as a template. IS will need to document the following:
- Current structure - will be technology based
- Shortcomings - usually in the area of clear definition of roles and responsibilities and centering on construction versus support
- Proposed structure - will be process based

c. IS Processes and IS Process Reengineering – Continued

The logical next step is to assign IS responsibility for the process steps and define roles and responsibilities. Using the new organization structure, this becomes fairly simple. Once IS management has aligned the process responsibility with the new organization structure, IS management can write roles and responsibilities. These ultimately spiral into IS job descriptions and the circle is complete. IS management has tied the strategy to the processes, the processes to the organization structure, the organization structure to the roles and responsibilities and the roles and responsibilities to the job descriptions. Another way of saying this is that we have aligned the strategy, the tactics and the individuals. The IS department is now organized to perform.

d. Technology Architecture

If IS management doesn't know where they are going, then any road will do. The last segment of the strategic trilogy is the technology architecture. It rounds out this strategic exercise and defines the strategic direction. It is the "what" portion of the strategy. This differs from the approach used in the business model strategy in one meaningful way. IS is no longer focusing on individual technologies but on the bigger picture of overriding architecture and the vision and principles needed to guide IS through the technology terrain. Here IS management has the opportunity to define the technology architecture and use the previous two strategic approaches to get them there.

The goals evolving around technology are to define a set of boundaries and guidelines against which technologies can be analyzed and fitted into the organization. It is a framework or external structure against which individual technologies, tools, languages and other attributes can be weighed. Using the analogy of a house, the technology architecture is the blueprint and the exterior framing. The individual technologies that are selected are the interior choices and the furniture.

The infrastructure or architecture engineering group within IS generally owns the architecture and must continually refine it and update it. They do this through a series of exercises and technology statements.

IS management and the IS infrastructure engineering group must prepare technology statements for each of the following components of the architecture:
- Data
- Platform
- Network
- Application
- Security
- Enterprise Management

These technology statements will be comprised of the following information:
- An introduction
- An executive summary
- Key issues and observations
- Assessment of current situation

- Architecture design principles
- Strategies
- Projects
- Standards and products
- Summary

The output of this exercise will be a technology architecture document. This should be a document that is kept current and frequently updated. IS infrastructure engineering needs to keep it current and available to the rest of the department.

The purpose of this strategy is to define the architecture planning process and to provide the architecture definition. IS management will then be able to define the technology architecture.

5. **Change Management Plan**

a. **Achieving Vision**

IS management has determined the "what," the "who," and the "how." Now comes the hard part. IS management must execute on the vision and change the organization. The vision from the strategy needs to be solidified and communicated to every employee throughout the course of every day until it eventually becomes a part of their daily work life. To accomplish this goal, at a minimum, the IS management must do the following:
- Develop and communicate slogans and buzzwords to create simple and consistent messages. For example, I find the "plan, build, run" slogan a useful one.
- Develop an internal IS marketing plan that holds the department leadership responsible and engages the associates.
- Look at each job in a different way and how each associate needs to act differently. Roles and responsibilities have changed and what worked in the past is no longer relevant.
- Focus on the processes and the process deliverables.

b. **Actions**

These are the actions that should be taken:
- IS management must gain acceptance of the strategy by both management and staff.
- IS must focus on the vision and on realizing that vision.
- IS management needs to focus on implementing the new organization and dealing with the chaos and grumbling that will follow.
- IS management must put the people first and remind them of the business imperative.
- IS must focus on process, process, process.
- The business must be assured that overall department performance will improve and IS must reference this fact frequently.

c. Resources Needed

IS management should be able to identify the tools and techniques that they need. These will include the following:
- IS management must market the vision and the changes and win the hearts and minds of the associates.
- It is imperative that every single business and IS management person buy into and participate in supporting change.
- The business should not be afraid to go outside for consulting assistance or business leadership participation.
- IS management must work hard to justify all funding with a promise of better service and more intelligent spending.
- IS management should always attempt to work within their budget.
- IS management should constantly think about their organization structure, how it is working and whether it needs to be adjusted.
- IS must focus on their customers (internal and external).

d. Timelines and Milestones

IS management must develop a rigid schedule with identifiable milestones. Again, think of the trilogy:
- Processes
- Organization
- Architecture

III. BUSINESS PROCESS STRATEGY SUMMARY

The business process strategy focuses on the trilogy of process, organization and architecture. It ties together strategy, tactics and the individual so that the strategy has real meaning.

Overcoming Growth Barrier 3   Chapter 11
Business Process Tactics

1. *Bring the business process strategy to fruition with solid tactics.*

2. *Process execution drives down to everything from projects to position descriptions.*

3. *The "Plan, Build, Run" organization structure works every time.*

4. *Use architecture statements to guide the technology selection process.*

I. INTRODUCTION

Armed with the new strategy, IS is ready to execute. The change management plan in the previous section is critical. Execution consists of a series of tactical moves and, in some cases, projects that will move the IS organization to the desired state. Strategies are made operational through implementation programs that are partitioned into projects.

IS leadership has to work on the following:
- The conclusions
- The critical issues
- The strategic moves in the areas of:
    - IS processes and IS process reengineering
    - Organization and realignment
    - Technology architecture
        - Data
        - Platform
        - Network
        - Application
        - Security
        - Enterprise Management

II. Execution on Processes

A. Skill Sets

IS personnel now require much more than just technology skill sets. Some of the skill sets of the existing IS staff have become either negotiable or obsolete. IS now needs less of the technology-centric technicians and more of the specialized process skill sets. Examples include great communication skills for the help desk, great problem-solving skills for second-level support, project management skills for that team and high-level engineering skills for the technology engineering team.

B. New Organization

The new organization should closely follow the model in appendix 10.5. IS management will need the simple "plan, build, run" terminology to explain it to the associates. It is nice to have a simple way to summarize the approach and to use as a mantra in explaining what the business and IS management is doing with the organization. I recommend a marketing campaign to sell the new vision to both the IS department and the business. It makes logical sense and I cannot emphasize enough the power in this simple structural change.

C. Position Descriptions

IS management needs to develop new position descriptions detailing roles and responsibilities. Instead of making this a dull and boring exercise, use it to reinforce and emphasize the vision. I have attached a couple of examples as appendices 11.1 and 11.2. Use these position descriptions to set the process expectation and reward the team when it is done properly.

D. Policies, Procedures and Standards (PPS)

The business and IS have an enormous amount of additional detailed work to do on PPS. The devil is in the details and these are the details in running a process focused department. I have listed a few of the required PPS below. IS management should quickly develop their own.
- Help desk contact procedures
- Help desk escalation flow and procedures
- Software development standards
- Infrastructure engineering technology diagrams
- IS recruiting process
- IS interviewing process
- Computer operations procedures and logs
- Change management procedures
- IS code of conduct policies
- Security policies and procedures

- Procurement policies and procedures
- Software acquisition standards

E. Structure

The structure of the reengineering effort must follow the "plan, build, run" model and looks like this:
- Where the plan encompasses planning and project management
- Where the build encompasses architecture engineering and software engineering
- Where the run encompasses computer operations and IS service and support

IS management needs to take each process and each group and define, in detail, the roles and responsibilities and the discreet process responsibilities. Refer to the PPS exercise above.

F. Projects

Begin with the plan groups and work through the run groups. Use the process responsibilities given above and the forms provided. Develop each of the exercises using the following approach:
- List the business processes (see the business model discussion)
- Match the related IS processes
- List any additional IS processes
- Document the IS processes
- Use the standard templates
- Review the IS processes
- Improve upon or eliminate the IS processes
- Publish the new processes

G. Forms

Please see the attached process and procedure templates found in appendix 10.3. These are workable templates. A process consulting resource may be able to improve on these.

H. Results

Here is where the business and IS management will see the major results of the process improvement efforts and the process improvements. Clear roles and responsibilities with documented and executed processes have an incredibly positive impact on both IS and the business. IS management will drastically improve both the communication and the accountability of the IS department. The IS process focus also removes many of the dependencies on individuals.

IS begins to focus on quantitative measurements instead of subjective opinions. IS management brings needed structure and methodology to the IS team. IS management implements ways to focus on return on investment (ROI) and other ways to support technology investments. IS begins to plan and not just react.

III. Execution on IS Organization and Realignment

A. Planning

Before this exercise can begin, IS management must rethink the entire organization and realignment exercise through to the end. IS management is attempting to retool the existing IS department in order to provide clear roles and responsibilities with a focus on process. IS management must pull the management team together, work through the details and gain total acceptance. Even one naysayer here can pull down and derail the entire effort. The business will have the most trouble with the IS technical management who still dabble in programming or technology solutions. If the business and IS management plans and executes properly, they will succeed. It is critical to recognize that IS cannot continue to function under the current organization structure.

B. Process Responsibilities

The new organization structure will be process driven. The best example I can give is in the area of infrastructure engineering. Let's take a telephony example. Let's say the business opens a new branch office and installs a new telephone system. All goes well and the technology at the branch comes up on schedule. All of the functionality is there and working. Days pass. There will be a myriad of daily service and support issues that will surface. They always do. The installation engineering team will initially handle these. After a while, however, two things will happen. First, the engineering team will get bored with the support issues and stop answering phone calls and emails. Engineers don't want to do support and post-installation support will naturally suffer. Second, the engineering team will move on to the next project. They will become engrossed in the new stuff and will stop responding to the support requests. Again, support will suffer. Now, in most cases, the success of the installation and the ongoing impression of the IS team is in the details. As the daily small support issues get ignored and missed, IS is basically throwing away opportunities to build the proper reputation and image for the IS department. Each interaction and each exchange is an opportunity. By leaving this to the installation engineers, who neither want nor can provide support, IS fails. The important point here is that support is a separate and distinct process from installation. Engineers should have process responsibility for installation. Support personnel must step in and provide the daily production support and seize the opportunity to properly support the business. Support should have responsibility for support.

C. Plan

The planning function is performed by the planning and project management department. They are responsible for keeping the long-range plans for the IS department. They set up standards and guidelines for planning and own the policies, procedures and standards. They execute and manage all projects, as well as assist the business in training on simple repeatable project management processes. Process responsibilities must include the following:

- Project identification
- Project compilation
- Project estimation (size and scope)
- Project management
- Project portfolio management
- Capital budgeting (optional)
- Project planning

D. Build

There are two distinct build groups. One builds the underlying infrastructure and the other builds or assembles the software and application systems that run on it.

1. Architecture Engineering

This group provides cost-effective technology solutions and third-tier technology support. They are a consulting resource as well as a research and development resource. They build the infrastructure, based on business requirements, to support existing and future applications. They are proactive, not reactive, and strive to do it right the first time. Process responsibilities must include the following:
- Develop infrastructure technology strategy
- Define and implement technology solutions
- Provide consulting services to the business (particularly sales)
- Provide infrastructure project management
- Provide third-tier technology support

2. Software Engineering

This group is a service driven organization that acquires, constructs and enhances the software and application technology solutions for the business. They are to acquire or build the appropriate software solutions through the use of appropriate methodologies. They must use published standards in the area of coding, testing, installation, documentation and user training. They are responsible for the following processes:
- Provide software acquisition
- Provide software construction
- Provide software enhancements
- Provide software project management
- Provide third-tier software support

E. Run

1. Computer Operations

This group focuses on running the production processes and managing the computer components on a daily basis. Their mission is to schedule, run and monitor

all aspects of the production computing environment. Some of these may vary from business to business. This includes everything that the build groups build. Once the infrastructure and applications are installed, responsibilities for these technologies are transferred to the computer operations group. They will ensure all resources are directed toward the timely and accurate completion of all production tasks. This includes scheduling, availability, performance, documentation, procedures, results, quality assurance and process management. Process responsibilities must include the following:
- Run installed infrastructure components
- Run installed application software components
- Manage any inputs and outputs
- Delivery of any produced products or services

2. User Service and Support

This group owns business user community communication–and sometimes customer user community communication–and first-tier technology break/fix. It is a service driven organization and is basically the voice of IS. They provide primary service and support to the users of technology. This includes anything that the build groups build and anything that the run group runs. Once the infrastructure and applications are installed, responsibility for all communications and break/fix activities are transferred to this group. They must ensure that all technologies are serviced and supported properly and that user relationships and expectations are managed properly. Process responsibilities must include the following:
- Maintain and manage user communication
- Manage technology break/fix
- Manage IS communication with customers, where applicable

IV. EXECUTION ON TECHNOLOGY ARCHITECTURE

Execution on technology architecture consists of using the architecture strategy and the architecture guidelines as IS continues to add to and expand the existing technology. IS management should use the technology statements when they are selecting technology. They should follow the guidelines. Complying with the direction and limitations developed in the strategy will allow IS to build a cohesive infrastructure and solution set to support the business. IS must leverage what they have developed. This is a consistent way to operate and it will save both time and money and allow IS to avoid costly mistakes.

V. SUMMARY

The business process tactics are geared toward bringing the trilogy of process, organization and architecture to fruition. Tactical execution is critical to realizing the vision and executing the strategy. The devil is in the details.

Overcoming Growth Barrier 3   Chapter 12
Business Process and the Individual

1. *This strategy will call for more specialists.*
2. *Package and market the company to be the right company for the employees.*
3. *Build the department to be the right department.*
4. *Select the right employees.*

I. INTRODUCTION

The business and the IS department will be severely challenged to build the process focused organization. The business may well be replacing a lot of the IS management and many of the IS associates. Technology managers generally hate process and do not want to give up doing for managing. Generalists do not want to become specialists. No one likes change. The business will be able to tell fairly quickly who is going to adapt and who is not. The changes will be painful but somewhat more manageable because the business leadership can be overt. The IS management will come to the business and express their hesitancy and concerns. This allows the business to deal with the difficult situation.

This is both a challenge and an opportunity. The business will find that they can go back to the basics and build a new IS department with a new focus and a renewed look at what is right. I summarize this work below by the emphasis on the following:
*   The right company
*   The right department
*   The right employee

II. BUSINESS PROCESS AND THE INDIVIDUAL

A. The Right Company

1. Core Values

To build the right kind of IS department, IS management needs to assure that this is the right company. By this I mean that the business needs to provide to the IS management a way to understand and embrace the core values of the company. Then IS management can make them known and relevant to the individual IS employee. If the IS executive can buy into and support the stated or unstated values, there is a strong chance that they can build the right IS organization. Stated core values emphasizing positive and honorable behavior cannot be overemphasized. IS management needs a solid foundation on which to build a team and this starts with the right core values and belief systems. To build the right department and to recruit the right individuals, IS management must feel they are working for the right company. I define the right company as one that make decisions and conducts business based on some inherent core values. The philosophy I am espousing is to build a working environment that incorporates and capitalizes on the best aspects of the company and its corporate culture.

2. Company Policies

To build the right kind of department and to stay in step with the corporate culture, IS management must closely review the company policies and procedures. The business and IS management must identify and determine, in advance, where these will need to be stretched or bent in some ways. IS associates are different and they work in a different environment. SMB company policies seldom address all of these differences. This is a delicate area in which to operate because adherence to policies must be balanced with creating the right IS environment for the associate. IS cannot be seen as a rogue department or support from human resources or other corporate support groups can dissipate. IS management must work closely with the business to create understanding and support for the differences in recruiting and retention that IS must face.

3. Company Culture

IS management and IS associates in SMBs are constantly interacting with every other associate in the business. From the executive team to the mailroom associate, IS management needs to establish a culture that services all levels of the company and all associates, regardless of rank, in an appropriate and consistent way. Given the proper core values, IS management must work to have the IS associates acting ethically and responsibly. There can be no untoward behavior or favoritism shown to individual users or various user groups. IS must service all groups equally and responsibly. IS management must reinforce the positive portion of the company culture and avoid participating in or reinforcing any negative aspects. In order to be effective and successful, the IS department must be above reproach.

B. The Right Department

1. Values

Given that the company core values and culture are positive enough and flexible enough, it becomes the total responsibility of the IS management team to build the right department based on the right values. It is important that IS management defines and agrees philosophically on the proper way to treat IS associates. IS management must educate IS associates about corporate politics and at the same time shield the associates from some of the certain harsh realities of the job. The goal here is to construct an environment of openness, honesty and trust. IS management must also learn to market the IS department to the IS department themselves by building a department based on values. That will make it easier to attract and retain the right associates.

2. Skills

The IS department is now large enough to need more IS specialists. The era of specialization increases even more under this model. Think of it as each associate wearing a skills tool belt. The new organization requires a totally different tool belt than associates would wear in the previous organization. Depending on the position, IS leadership needs to be concerned with the following:

- Technical skills
    - o Understanding of relevant hardware, software or other technology
    - o Understanding of technical concepts, principles and underlying technologies
    - o Ability to assimilate new information
    - o Staying abreast of current trends, future trends and literature
    - o Assuring self-training
    - o Understand and practice matching technology to business needs
- Communication skills
    - o Verbal
    - o Written
    - o Presentation
- Work habits
    - o Quantity of work
    - o Quality of work
    - o Attendance and punctuality
    - o Planning and organization
    - o Customer service focus
- Personal traits
    - o Appearance
    - o Confidence and poise
    - o Attitude
    - o Spirit of cooperation
    - o Critical thinking and decision making
    - o Dependability and discipline
    - o Initiative
    - o Creativity and resourcefulness
    - o Leadership ability
    - o Supports affirmative action
    - o Problem-solving ability
    - o Achievement-oriented
- Prior education and training
    - o Formal education

- Adult or follow-up education
- Previous training
- Previous experience

3. Attitudes

One of the personal traits warrants being singled out for additional discussion. I am talking about attitude. That intangible cannot be overemphasized. It is critical that IS management recruit, retain and sustain associates with the right attitude. The industry standard is that "the customer is king" and nowhere is this more appropriate than in the SMB IS organization. There are numerous opportunities for the IS organization to expound on this philosophy through their behaviors whether it be answering the phone, walking through a department or supporting the senior business leadership.

C. The Right Employee

1. Recruiting

The following guidelines should be used for identifying, scheduling, interviewing and hiring the right employee. In many SMBs, the recruiting process is often haphazard and poorly conceived. IS management should strive to provide structure for this process. The guidelines focus on the proper way to run the recruiting process and the proper way to evaluate and select employees. It is critical that IS management comply with corporate human resource policies and procedures and supplement these with their own.

The exercise of recruiting is critical to long-term IS success. IS wins or loses with people. The best organization structure in the world will not succeed without the right people. The process of recruiting needs to be so well-defined that the process works independently and without ownership. Each hiring or interviewing manager needs to know the process and the forms involved and remember to complete their responsibilities. I divide the recruiting process into three major procedures:
- Preparation and screening
- Interviewing
- Offers

Quickly make sure the budget, the job description, the salary guidelines, the approved position and the human resource requirements are defined and fulfilled. IS management should document these and educate the staff to comply with them.

One of the most critical components of recruiting is the initial screening. IS management should learn to read a resume and classify an employee in various ways. Ask all hiring managers and interviewers to assist in the screening process. Devise an interview screening form. The goal here is to gather information about the candidate and the possible future fit with the department and the working environment. Documentation is critical. I have seen employers waste time interviewing the same candidate multiple times due to poor record keeping. I have also seen good employees slip through the recruiting net because the employer could not intelligently evaluate the worthiness of their talent.

The interview procedure itself can also be structured and geared toward collecting and retaining as much information about the candidate as possible. This procedure involves the following:
- Scheduling
- Participation
- Forms
- Interviews
- Documenting results
- Offer/No offer decisions

For scheduling, IS management can devise a simple form that sets up the interview schedule and structures the interview process. They will find it valuable for all interviewers to work from a common schedule since emergencies often arise and force juggling of the sequence of the interviewers. IS management should use at least three and no more than five interviewers. Less than three and the result will be not enough data to go on. More than five and the process becomes repetitive and unwieldy. IS management should have both IS management and senior members of the IS staff participate. IS management needs the line employees to feel like they are part of the recruiting and selection process. IS management should also want the candidate to understand that they expect full disclosure by both parties and that the process is entirely open and honest. IS management should also advise the interviewers to be as candid as possible with their responses. All businesses and all IS departments have problems and challenges in their working environments and a savvy candidate knows this. The goal should be to get the candidate to decide to work on this particular set of business problems and challenges.

Now that the candidate and interviewers are scheduled, IS management will conduct the interview. There are numerous superior books on interviewing. Please read up on interviewing tips and techniques or work with someone with solid skills in this area. Please work with human resources or self-teach the laws regarding interviewing and the areas that IS interviewers should not and cannot delve into. These rules and regulations change as a result of court cases and findings so IS interviewers must take great pains to understand the candidate's rights and their responsibilities. IS management can devise an interview results form to record the outcome of the interview. The content of this form will vary based on the working environment and management experiences. It is imperative that each interviewer fill out the interview results form at the time of the interview or immediately after the interview is concluded. If IS is interviewing several candidates then memory will not serve.

The decision to make an offer comes as a consensus decision among the interviewers. Each interviewer will come away from the session with a different feeling about the candidate. The IS management job is to distill from the interview results form the essence of the candidate as a potential employee. IS management can conduct a post-interview meeting where the candidate can be candidly discussed and a recommendation reached. It is important that IS management also use this time to evaluate the reviewers. Look for negative or positive trends or where the interviewer reached an evaluation or opinion quite different from the rest of the group. This can be valuable insight or signs of a flawed interviewer. During the post-interview stage, and prior to any offer, ask questions about the candidate to see how well the candidate's potential is understood. Focus on not just the basics but what other skill sets and experiences IS may get, regardless of the current organizational structure. The offer process needs to be handled by human resources, if possible. Remember that this will be a negotiation session and that IS needs to continue to sell the company, the department and themselves. While salary will be important to the candidate so will the working environment, the technology, the challenge and the day-to-day work life of the employee.

2. Retention

The key to staff retention is staying in constant touch with each employee and dealing with their day-to-day "me" issues before these become critical. IS management may do this through associate one-on-one meetings and through an accountability manual. The accountability manual is a formal approach that attempts to hold both the manager and the employee responsible for the employee's future employment. The manager is responsible for communicating with the employee and dealing productively with the employee's feelings and attitudes. The employee is responsible for their own career and for giving their manager the opportunity to make the work experience an enjoyable and productive one. Both need to be held accountable.

In practice, to make this happen, each manager should spend fifteen minutes each week with each subordinate in a one-on-one meeting situation. The discussion needs to be centered on the following topics that correspond to sections in the accountability manual.

From the manager's perspective:
- Performance on tasks shown as quality of work
- Performance on deadlines shown as quantity of work
- Adherence to policies, procedures and standards
- Attendance and punctuality
- Customer service focus
- Planning and organizing
- Other observations

From the employee's perspective:
- Feelings about the work
- Feelings about the company
- Benefits and compensation
- Training
- The future including career and job growth

IS management should expect each manager to develop and maintain an accountability manual for each employee. This can be a physical paper-based manual or an electronic record-keeping manual. The accountability manual has three major sections:
- Expectations
- Performance
- Training and Enrichment

These should be discussed during each employee's one-on-one session. Each session should be concluded with notes from both the manager and the associate to continually document status and progress.

3. Training

I single out this issue to emphasize the importance IS management should place on cultivating a learning environment and providing options for training that may better suit the usual small training budget. IS management may conduct an exercise where the goals and aspirations of the associate are documented through the accountability manual and action plans are developed to make those goals a reality. These goals will inevitably include a training component. IS doesn't have to spend real dollars on training but they do have to spend real time, energy and effort. Alternate training options are always available and include mentoring, research opportunities, in-house devised training courses and one-on-one sessions with knowledgeable individuals from within the business. If there is one issue that every IS individual shares, it is the issue of training. More so than with pay or benefits, retention can be vastly improved with training.

III. SUMMARY

To succeed with this strategy the business will need more specialized skill sets and, more than likely, different individuals. Skill set mapping is a worthwhile exercise. Many employees cannot subscribe to a process focus. Make every effort to align the work environment to have the right company, the right department and the right individuals. Recruiting, retention and training are all equally important.

The Ten Commandments of IT Strategy

WISDOM to work by:

1. *You must never develop software from scratch.*

2. *You must never buy a software package and make modifications to it.*

3. *You must never look for a competitive edge in your infrastructure.*

4. *You must never look for a competitive edge in your back office.*

5. *You must always align your technology models with your business model.*

6. *You must always document your IT strategic areas of focus.*

7. *You must always remember your IT strategic drivers.*

8. *You must always establish your IT strategic teams.*

9. *You must always establish an IT council.*

10. *You must know the strategic trilogy*

I. INTRODUCTION

The best way to summarize this book is to take the key points from each strategy and create a guide book of sorts. I have chosen the ten commandments format as a memorable way to summarize and present the accumulated wisdom of the strategies.

II. COMMANDMENT NUMBER 1

You must never develop software from scratch.

There is no good business reason for developing software from scratch anymore. The SMB usually cannot spare the time it takes to develop software since this is inevitably a long-term solution. I would go further and say that if any SMB now has active software development projects where they are coding the application from scratch, they should immediately stop. Even if the project appears to be 90 percent done, I would recommend immediate closure. This is a bold statement I know. But I honestly believe there is not a business case for developing software from scratch anymore. Nearly everyone has seen the iceberg diagram where the vast majority of the iceberg is under water and below the water line. The mass above the line represents development and the much larger mass below the surface represents maintenance and support. That is the commitment a business is making when they begin a software development project. Another important reason for not developing software from scratch is that the majority of software development projects fail. Whatever source of reference or statistics one uses, it can be shown that up to 80 percent of all software development projects fail. This includes projects in even the largest companies with nearly unlimited resources. By fail I mean they do not come in on time, do not come in within budget or do not deliver the target functionality.

To me, software development is a no-win situation. So the natural question to ask is: how does the SMB get software? I would answer that to get software for the back office applications, the business should buy it. For customer facing applications, the business should buy it or build it using components or tool kits. I also recommend exploring an ASP (application service provider) or SaaS (Software as a Service) solutions.

III. COMMANDMENT NUMBER 2

Commandment number 2 is also software related.

You must never buy a software package and make modifications to it.

Buying software and internally making modifications to that software is a huge software technology trap. The SMB buys a package and immediately finds it is missing some functionality that someone in the organization feels they cannot live without. Stop! Don't do it! Don't modify it! One of two things has happened. One— and by far the leading case—the SMB has bought the wrong software package. Most SMBs do not know how to go through a structured and rigorous software selection process. Two, the SMB is trying to force the software to match the internal business processes instead of modifying the internal business processes to meet the require-ments of the software. What difference does it make to your customers how you process your business internally? The answer is none. Why not change the internal processes? The answer is usually because the existing staff is rigid and inflexible. This software technology trap is avoidable. If the SMB does a sound and thorough job of software application selection and they are flexible in their internal business processes they can find a package that works out of the box and without customization. Violation of this commandment leads to many problems. The SMB becomes out of step with the vendor. The SMB cannot take new versions and new releases with-out severe consternation. It also ties the business to the package forever at a weaker version.

IV. COMMANDMENT NUMBER 3

You must never look for a competitive edge in your infrastructure.

Please remember that when I say infrastructure I mean all of the hardware components such as networks, servers and telephone systems. I am taking about all of the physical technology components—the stuff you can touch. Business people should never have to hear about this stuff, ever. To them, these technologies should be exactly like utilities—just like electricity. You flip the switch and the lights come on. You don't hear business people talk about power generators and relay stations and volts and wattage. It just works. So should your infrastructure! When the business person uses the network they should not have to consider bandwidth and security and file sizes and transmission speeds. They should just be able to use it. Period! You need to get your infrastructure built, preferably by leveraging external integrators, have one person manage the relationships and delivery of the services and forget about it. It should just work! Infrastructure is a "me too" proposition. You either have it and you can do business or you don't and you can't. It provides no competitive edge. It really does nothing for your customers.

V. COMMANDMENT NUMBER 4

You must never look for a competitive edge in your back office.

Just like infrastructure, back office expenditures are a cost of doing business. Remember back office applications are predominantly the software systems and applications you need to do business on a daily basis. These applications are surprisingly common from business to business. These, too, should just work and should work as purchased out of the box. If you have to customize or tweak the code then you bought the wrong tool. One of the biggest problems in any IT organization is buying the wrong packages. There are ways to ensure that you buy the right package by doing a thorough job on requirements and following a solid methodology. The back office has all been built by someone else. You don't want to sacrifice the opportunity cost when you could be spending your time on customer facing applications. As with infrastructure, these applications need to just work and provide the required functionality. Again, like a utility. There is nothing here that benefits your customers that the competition is not already doing. While poor back office applications not done properly can ruin your business, they cannot differentiate you with your customers. If they can, then they are not really back office applications but customer facing ones.

Look outward, not inward.

VI. COMMANDMENT NUMBER 5

You must always align your technology models with your business model.

Most businesses have not taken the time to document their business or technology models. This can be a galvanizing exercise. You can depict the business model in a simple one-page flowchart or one-page business flow. It starts with the marketing and sales process, moves through delivery of the product or service and culminates with receivables and revenue. A technology model is simply multiple views encompassing the software, hardware and networking components of the company. It is the way the IT team has constructed their technology solutions to meet the business needs. By mapping the technology models over the top of the business model, the SMB can hone in on the technologies that are critical and relevant to the business. By comparing these two models, the business can come up with some startling conclusions. The SMB can see where there are misalignments and bottlenecks. More importantly, the SMB can identify those broad technology areas the business should be considering. I believe there exists a commonality among businesses where certain foundational building blocks of software applications have already been built. You simply need to purchase the components and integrate them to support your business. I am talking about broad functional technologies like work flow, document management, call center management or distribution applications. This is where I back up my statements about not doing software development from scratch. A better alternative is to buy these components or building blocks and configure or integrate them in creative and unique ways to meet specific business needs.

VII. COMMANDMENT NUMBER 6

You must always document your IT strategic areas of focus.

This commandment is critical. Your strategic areas of focus are the core broad technology areas identified when the SMB maps the technology models to the business model in the previous exercise. These are the fundamental building blocks of all customer facing applications. The business must clearly identify and document these technology areas. The business can then build on these strategic areas of focus and identify the right technology projects. These are the tool kits and broad applications that the business will buy and integrate to deliver services to customers. Without knowing this basic information—these strategic areas of focus—the business is at the whims of the technology or operational groups for project identification and technology investments. Without using strategic areas of focus, the chances are good that the business will not invest in the right technology and will be doing the wrong projects.

Strategic areas of focus give the business a fresh perspective and allow the SMB to invest in the right technologies. Strategic areas of focus can get the business back on the right technology track.

VIII. COMMANDMENT NUMBER 7

You must always remember your IT strategic drivers.

Within the strategic areas of focus, there must be some rules and regulations about how to select technology solutions from the many choices that are available. I call these strategic drivers and they vary from business to business. These IT strategic drivers should dictate what is important and relevant when selecting specific technology solutions. These are the guiding principles for technology selection. A good example of a strategic driver would be a statement like this:

"Due to our company focus on customer service, our technology and systems will be flexible enough to enable customization based on the specific needs of each customer. We cannot afford to take a mass production approach because our customers require different solutions based on their particular circumstances. It is expensive to acquire and maintain customers so we must guard them carefully. Our competitors are customizing. In order to be competitive we must also customize."

In this case, one of the strategic drivers becomes customization for each customer. These drivers will guide in selecting technology and provide a yardstick against which to measure technology selections. The right drivers lead to the right technology choices.

IX. COMMANDMENT NUMBER 8

You must always establish IT strategic teams.

IT strategic teams are teams comprised of both business leaders and IT professionals and are managed or chaired by a business leader. I have been in this field for a long time so I can safely say the following: you cannot leave management of technology or technology projects solely to IT. It just doesn't work. Besides, there are no IT projects, only business projects that may have a huge technology component. At worst, you need a business owner and an IT owner with the IT person reporting to the business person. Each IT strategic team is generally responsible for a single strategic area of focus such as work flow or call center technologies. The IT strategic team is tasked with:
- Project identification
- Project selection
- Project scoping
- Project sequencing
- Execution of the projects that fall out of the focus area

The IT strategic teams become the subject matter experts and the owners of the business segment involved. Their challenge is to deliver on the focus area and assure that the technology dollars are spent on the right technology projects.

X. COMMANDMENT NUMBER 9

You must always establish an IT council.

An IT council is responsible for seeing that the strategy gets implemented. Once the business has selected a strategy, it needs a group of senior executives who understand and can implement the strategy. They are responsible for the tactics. The business needs to control IT projects and the IT strategic teams. This council will broker the needs of the various IT strategic teams. This group needs to be firmly entrenched in the decision-making process. They must select appropriately from all of the technology projects that need to be done. They need to set the priorities, expect the deliverables and make the tough choices. This council needs to fund and support the various initiatives. Without an IT council—if you'll pardon the expression—the inmates are running the asylum.

XI. COMMANDMENT NUMBER 10

You must know the strategic trilogy.

Once the business and the IS department gets to be a specific size, and once the selected strategy has solved some of the problems that it will solve, the business will need to focus on the strategic trilogy. These are the three areas that will provide the most challenges as both the business and the IS department grow. These three areas are easily remembered as the strategic trilogy.
- Process
- Organization
- Architecture

The IS department will grow to the point where technology will not be an impediment but internal processes will. Processes will be broken and will need to be revamped. The SMB must institute a process focus.

The IS department will have the wrong organization structure resulting in roles and responsibilities that are not clearly defined. There will be overlap and confusion. IT service will be lousy with even the simplest requests not being satisfied. The IS department will need to organize around process instead of around technologies.

The SMB will be taking a narrow view of technology with resulting solutions that will not grow or scale. The SMB will need to get into architectural considerations and how best to structure larger solution sets. The SMB will need to write architecture statements.

XII. SUMMARY

No matter what the chosen strategy, do not violate these commandments lightly. There are exceptions to every rule and sometimes there will be good business reasons to disregard one but try to follow these ten commandments.

WISDOM to work by:

1. *Most SMBs will hit the three barriers described herein as they grow.*

2. *The three strategies offered will remove those barriers.*

3. *Select a strategy and write it down.*

4. *Use the tools and templates provided when possible.*

5. *IT is really not about the technology.*

6. *IT is really about the strategy.*

I have identified three major IS barriers and offered three strategic approaches to surmount them. The missing component in most IS organizations is the strategy. However one defines strategy, knowing where the business and IS wants to go and charting a path to get there is absolutely critical. Writing it down and focusing on it makes a real difference. If one were to go into any IS department and assume they have a shared vision and concurrence on a strategic direction, it would be a serious mistake. It is impossible to align the tactics and the personnel to an undefined strategy. If a business skips this step, they lose. I am convinced that merely buying and using this book will give a business a competitive edge. The competition will be viewing their barriers as technology and personnel challenges, while your business will be viewing them as strategic challenges. The competition will be thrashing around and assessing blame. Your business will be accepting the inevitable and moving toward solutions. Your business will beat the competition through the next hurdle.

This book references numerous tools and templates. I have chosen not to include all of them. If your business or IS leadership needs any of the additional tools or templates noted in this book, feel free to contact me directly. I fully intend to make these available through a website for anyone attending one of my seminars or purchasing my book.

I also wish to reiterate that this book is based on my more then forty years of experience in technology and leverages my observations and those of my colleagues. I would encourage the reader to share dissimilar experiences and observations with me. I would like to build on this body of work and I am open to improving these processes and methodology where possible.

And last, paraphrasing an old saying, those who fail to learn from the mistakes of the past are doomed to repeat them. This could not be more true than when addressing IS issues in SMBs. I have seen numerous executives in SMBs who feel the problems and challenges identified in this book are unique to their company or their industry. This could not be further from the truth. These are not new barriers or unique situations. These are common and universal plights. The missing component is that no one has leveraged the experience of others because no one has found the proper forum. This book is an attempt to pass along some of the accrued wisdom and experience of myself and others. I am confident that any SMB will benefit from it. IT is not about the technology. IT is about the strategy.

IT is about the Strategy

Appendix

Appendix I-1

IT Barriers and Strategic Solutions

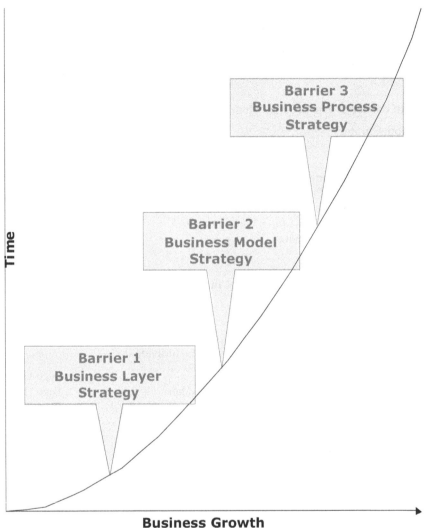

Appendix 2-1

Business Layer Strategy and Tactics

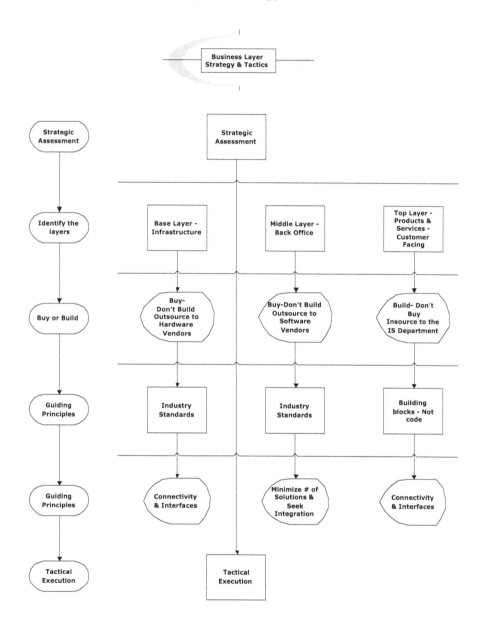

Appendix 2-2

Business Layer Approach - Technology Assessment

Customers

Customer Facing Applications

Back Office Applications

Infrastructure

Appendix 6-1

Business Model Strategy

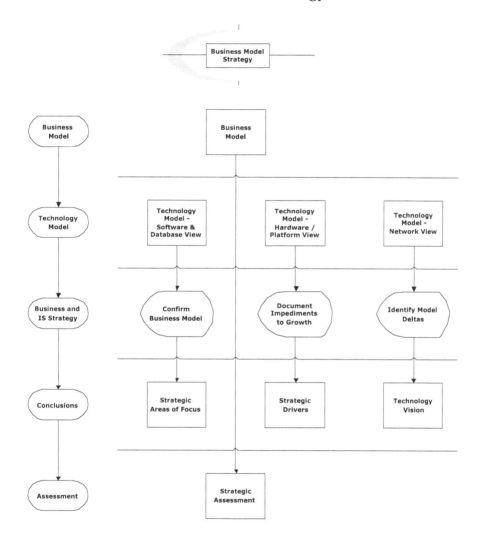

Appendix 6-2

Business Model Tactics

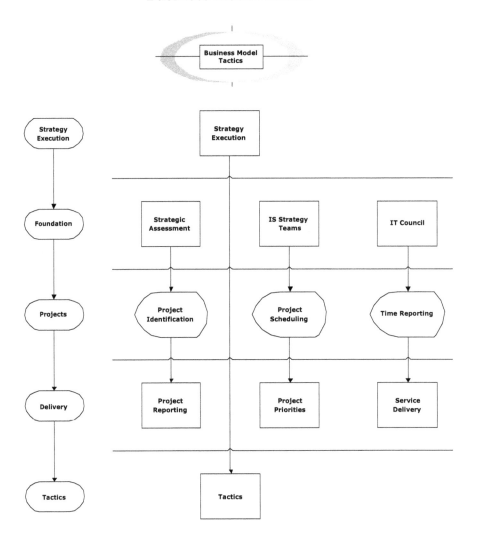

Appendix 6-3

Sample Business Model

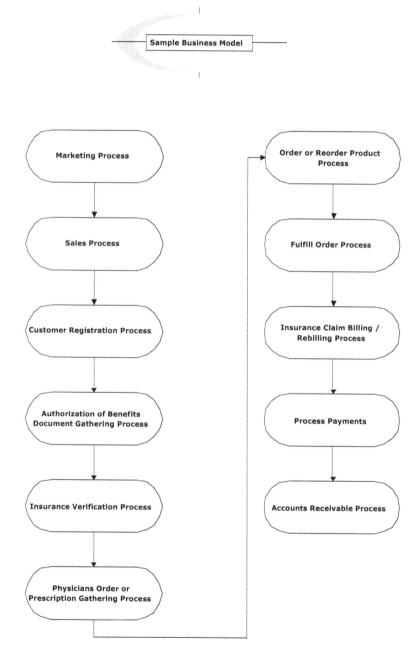

Appendix 6-4

Sample Business Model Authorization of Benefits

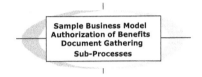

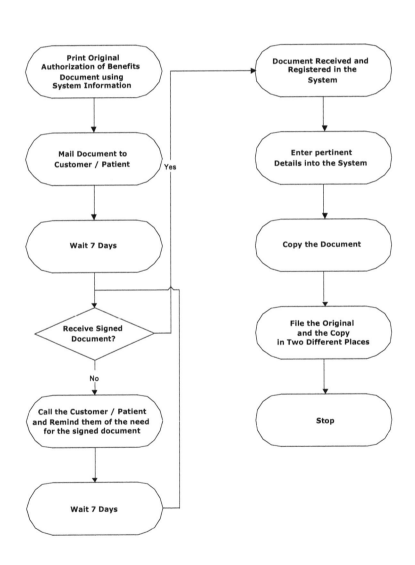

Appendix 6-5

Sample Software and Database Model View

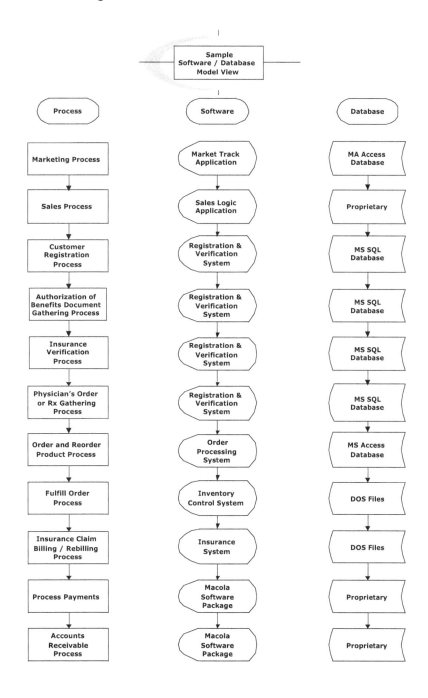

Appendix 6-6

Sample Hardware and Platform Model View

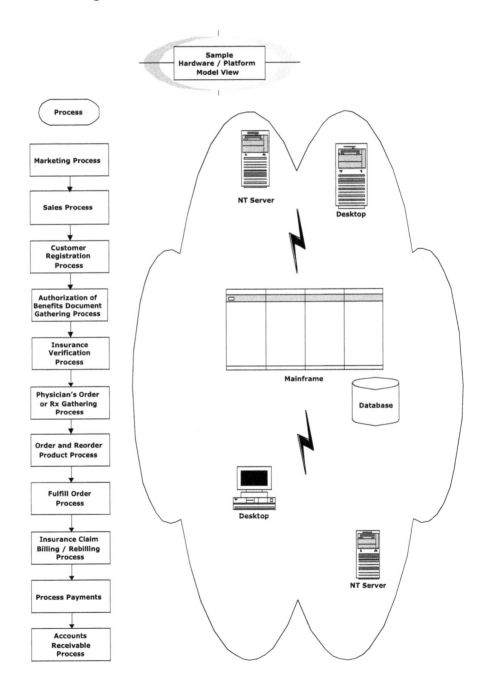

Appendix 6-7

Sample Software Technology Vision

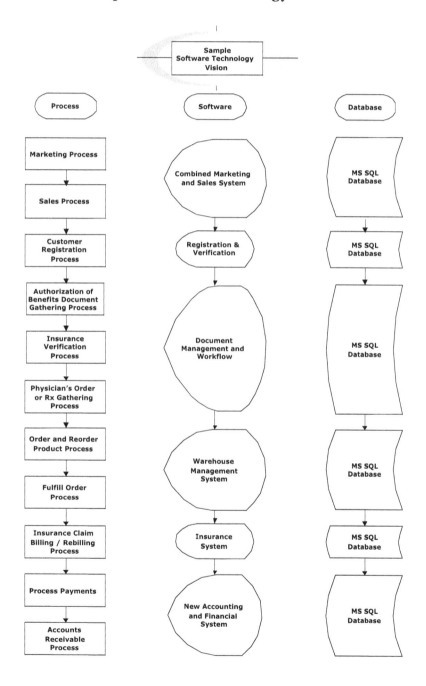

Appendix 7-1

Maintain IS Project List

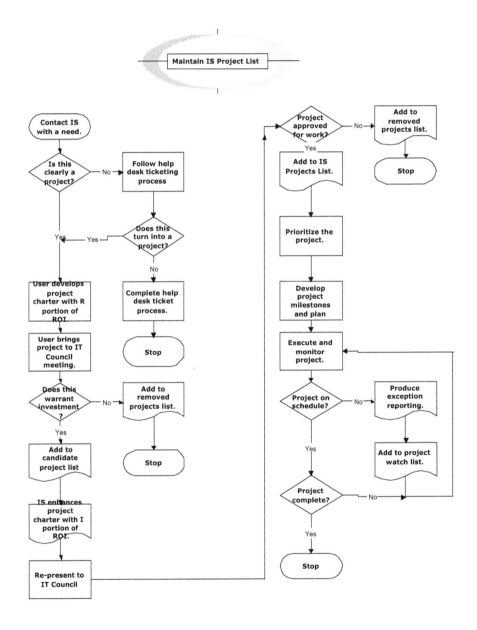

Appendix 8-1

IS Service Pyramid

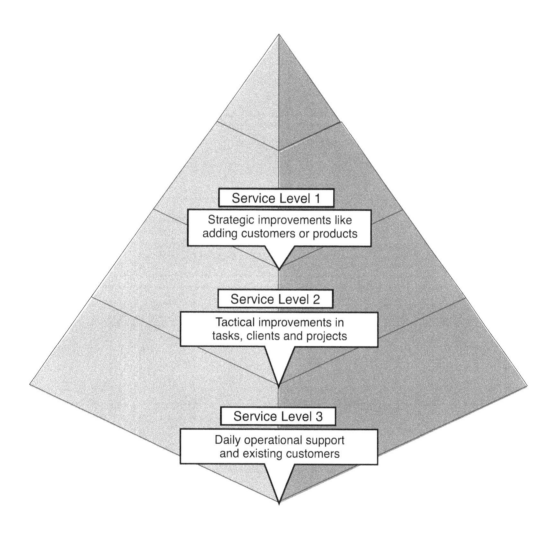

Appendix 8-2

Sample Daily Systems Availability Communication Plan

#	Message	Audience	Frequency	Responsibility	Vehicle	Intent
1	Nightly Batch Processing Successful	Entire Company	Daily M-F	Computer Operations	Green Light Symbol on the Intranet Home Page	All things normal
2	Nightly Batch Processing Did Not Complete Successfully	Entire Company	Daily M-F Prior to 8:00 AM	Computer Operations	Yellow Light Symbol on the Intranet Home Page	Report a problem and focus on resolution.
		Management	Daily M-F Prior to 8:00 AM or when a problem occurs	Computer Operations	Morning Incident Report w/1 hour updates to management via email	Report a problem and focus on resolution.
3	Nightly Batch Processing Did Not Complete Successfully - Problem Resolved	Entire Company	Daily M-F within 1 hours of resolution	Computer Operations	Green Light Symbol on the Intranet Home Page	All things normal
		Management	Daily M-F within 1 hours of resolution	Computer Operations	Incident report filed on shared drive within 24 hours of resolution	All things normal

Batch

Appendix 8-2

Sample Daily Systems Availability Communication Plan (continued)

Systems

#	Message	Audience	Frequency	Responsibility	Vehicle	Intent
4	All Systems Available	Entire Company	Daily M-F	Computer Operations	Green Light Symbol on the Intranet Home Page	All things normal
6	Daily Production System not Available	Entire Company	Daily M-F Prior to 8:00 AM	Computer Operations	Yellow Light Symbol on the Intranet Home Page	Report a problem and focus on resolution.
		Management	Daily M-F Prior to 8:00 AM or when a problem occurs	Computer Operations	Morning Incident Report w/1 hour updates to management via email	Report a problem and focus on resolution.
7	Daily Production System not Available - Problem Resolved	Entire Company	Daily M-F within 1 hours of resolution	Computer Operations	Green Light Symbol on the Intranet Home Page	All things normal
		Management	Daily M-F within 1 hours of resolution	Computer Operations	Incident report filed on shared drive within 24 hours of resolution	All things normal
8	Problem with Batch Processing or Systems Availability that exceed one day	Management	Daily M-F when a problem exceeds one day	Director of IS	Incident Report via e-mail message each hour	Daily status report and daily impact statement

Appendix 8-3

Sample IS Scorecard

Yearly Goal	Q2 Goal	Q2 Key Measure	Resp. Party	Current Status	Possible Score	Score
Strategy Definition	Develop strategies (3) for Document Management, Billing, and Distribution.	Publish Strategies.				
	Document Management	Strategy	RPS	Y	5	5
	Billing	Strategy	RPS	Y	5	5
	Distribution	Strategy	RPS	N	5	0
Systems/Service Availability	Develop method for tracking on Systems/Service availability.	Publish monthly report.	DF	Y	10	10
Service Level Agreements	"Existing Customer" (internal business user) service.	Install Service Level Agreement tracking through "Track IT".	DF	Y	10	10
Performance on Projects	Performance on Projects:					
	1. Successful Delivery of internal Projects					
	Compliance Project	Completed Project.	BM	Y	10	10
	CVA Project	Completed Project.	BM	Y	10	10
	2. Successful Delivery of Infrastructure Projects:	Complete 1 out of 1 project.	BM	Y	5	5
	3. Successful Delivery New Development Projects:	Complete 8 out of 11 projects.	All	9 of 11	10	10
	4. Define acquisition integration solutions.	Written report and acceptance.	All	Y	10	10
Performance within Budget						
	Performance within manpower Budget.	Manpower expenditures = to or below budget.	All	Y	20	20
		Totals			**100**	**95**

Appendix 10-1

Business Process Strategy

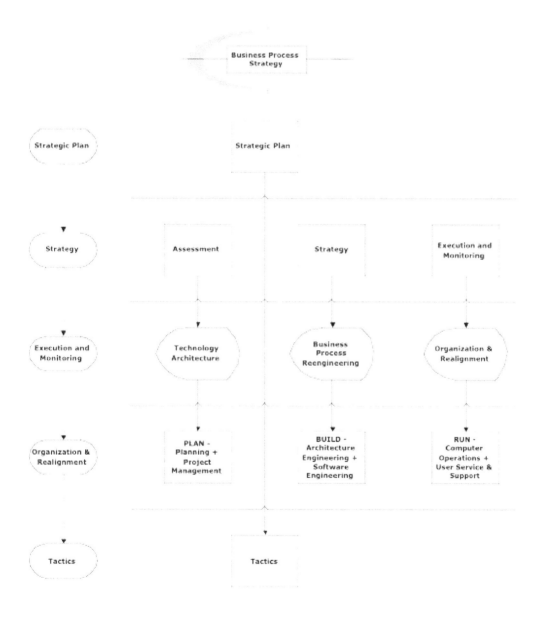

Appendix 10-2

Alignment Excercise

Aligned?	Business	Applications Development	Systems Administration	Procurement	Telecom	Desktop Support
Applications Development	No-1	NA	No-5	Yes	Yes	No-6
Systems Administration	No-2	No-5	NA	Yes	Yes	No-7
Procurement	Yes	Yes	Yes	NA	Yes	Yes
Telecom	No-3	Yes	Yes	Yes	NA	Yes
Desktop Support	No-4	No-6	No-7	Yes	Yes	NA

No-1	Applications Development does not do a good job on software requirements. They also do not train the business users well. The business misuses the systems by putting data in the wrong fields.

No-2	Systems Administration does not communicate planned outages well. They do not publish and adhere to maintenance windows. The business will try to use the system during planned outages.

No-3	Telecom cannot keep up with the number of changes in the call center. The business does not notify telecom of changes in a timely manner.

No-4	Desktop Support services PCs when users are absent. Users PCs stop working or work differently and they do no know why. Users try to load unlicensed software and unapproved screen savers.

No-5	Applications Development does not feel that they have all of the rights and privileges they need to do their jobs. Systems Administration feels that Applications Development writes inefficient code and sap system resources unnecessarily.

No-6	Desktop Support complains that Applications Development loads unlicensed software and fools with PC settings. Applications Development feels that Desktop Support locks down PCs too tightly and that it gets in the way of development.

No-7	Systems Administration feels that Desktop support does not follow their instructions when setting up work stations. Desktop Support must do some installations without proper documentation.

Appendix 10-3

Sample Process Template

Process Name:
Process ID:
Version:
Effective Date:
Process Owner:
Scope:
Definition of process:
Reasons for process:

Supporting Documents:

Supporting Procedures:

Procedure #:	Procedure Name:
1001	
1002	
1003	
1004	
1005	

Roles:

Process:

Responsible party: **Process step:**

Appendix 10-3

Sample Procedure Template

Procedure:
Procedure ID:
Version:
Effective Date:
Key Contact:
Parent Process:

Process Name:	Process #:

Scope:
Functional Participants:

Participants:

Procedure Steps:

Materials Needed:

Responsible   **Task**

Appendix 10-4

Technology Based Organization

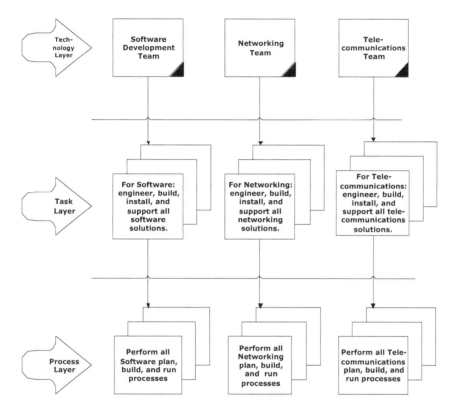

Appendix 10-5

Process Based Organization

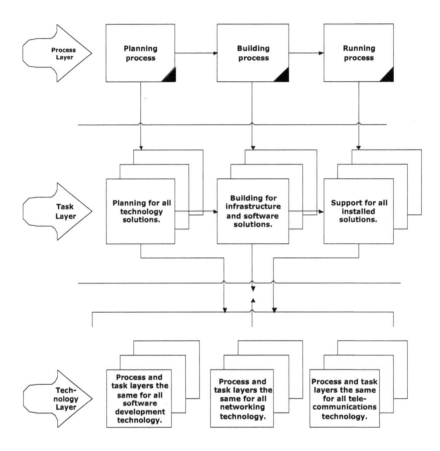

Appendix 11-1

Sample Job Description 1

Position Description
Technology Support Analyst II

Roles and Responsibilities:
The Technology Support Analyst II contributes to the success of the Information Services Delivery/Support function by installing, supporting, monitoring, testing and troubleshooting the hardware and software pertaining to one or more of the Company's voice, data and desktop technology platforms. The Technology Support Analyst II should demonstrate a proficient understanding of at least two technology platforms (voice, data, desktop) and easily performs Level I and Level II problem determination on the platforms. The position relies on a strong technical aptitude and sound judgment to accomplish goals. The function is expected to perform a variety of tasks concurrently.

Requisite Skills:
Technical - Must have a proficient understanding of two of the three technology platforms identified above (voice, data, desktop).
Communication - Must have excellent communication skills, verbal and written.
Management - The Technology Analyst II has no supervisor responsibility.
Mentoring - Must mentor and enrich the professional lives of junior IS associates. Must deal with all employees showing dignity and respect.
Projects - Must understand standard project management methodology and perform tasks as outlined in project plans.
Service - Must have a customer service mentality for both internal and external customers.
Relevant Experience: Minimum of 2-5 years of experience in a mid size technology diverse, multi-tasking environment. Most recent experience should include one year in a role where the primary responsibility is technology support and implementation.
Education: Required - A+ Certification, equivalent industry experience
                      Preferred - Technical school diploma, MCSE
Reports To: Manager Technology Support, Director Technology Support, or VP Technology Support

Performance Measurements:
Support –Performance measurements will include the number of Help Desk Tickets resolved, timeliness of resolution, update status of tickets, and quality of problem resolution.
Administration – Performance measurements will include adherence to IS standards and procedures including time recording, and asset management.
Projects - Performance measurements will include implementation of project tasks on time / within budget / and with full functionality, adherence to project management methodology, adherence to documentation and procedures standards.
Process – Performance measurements will include adherence to IS Support policies and procedures including cabling, configuration, tape backups, security, and licensing.

Allocation of Time:

Construction:	20%
Service/Support:	70%
Project Management:	10%

Appendix 11-2

Sample Job Description 2

Position Description
Help Desk Manager

Roles and Responsibilities: Responsible for the Level 1 support process within the Delivery / Support function of Information Services. Develops the Level 1 support process vision for the organization. Assembles and maintains a team of Help Desk analysts. Designs and constructs the Help Desk processes and procedures to meet the needs of the business.

Requisite Skills:

Technical – Must understand and show proficiency with the underlying technology.

Communication – Must have excellent communication skills, verbal and written, and solid presentation skills.

Leadership – Must be able to lead people toward a common goal and develop a team approach.

Management – Must be able to manage numerous Level 1 support processes simultaneously without deterioration of service delivery.

Mentoring – Must mentor and enrich the professional lives of employees. Must deal with all employees showing dignity and respect.

Projects – Must adopt understand standard project management methodology and define and document repeatable processes.

Service - Must have a customer service mentality for both internal and external customers.

Relevant Experience: 5-7 years in progressive leadership positions.

Education: Required – Associate or technical degree, or comparable certifications
               Preferred – Bachelors degree

Reports To: VP Information Services Delivery

Performance Measurements:

Administration – Performance measurements will include development and communication of the Level 1 support process vision, leadership and team building, mentoring and employee development, understanding and projection of a service mentality.

Projects – Performance measurements include technical appropriateness of service solutions, delivery of projects on time / within budget / and with full functionality, adherence to project management methodology, adherence to documentation and procedures standards.

Process – Performance measurements will include ability to standardize, document, and develop means for institutionalizing repeatable processes and instilling a process approach within the team.

Allocation of Time:

Construction:	10%
Service/Support:	70%
Project Management:	20%

www.ingramcontent.com/pod-product-compliance
Lightning Source LLC
Chambersburg PA
CBHW080423060326
40689CB00019B/4353